DANIEL AS A BLUEPRINT FOR NAVIGATING ETHICAL DILEMMAS (2ND EDITION)

ETHICAL LEADERSHIP ACROSS TIME

RICHARD FRENCH

Indie Pen Press

Turning Dreams Into Best Sellers

Indie Pen Press
Seattle, Washington USA
IndiePenPress.com

Second Edition: June 2025

Paperback ISBN 979-8-9919463-9-1

CONTENTS

PREFACE: ETHICAL LEADERSHIP IN A COMPLEX WORLD

A moment forever changed my understanding of ethical leadership. I sat across from a brilliant executive who had just been forced to resign from his C-suite position at a major company. His career lay in shambles, his reputation tarnished, the weight of his choices visible in his posture.

"I never saw it coming," he told me, his voice barely above a whisper. "There wasn't one big moment where I chose to compromise my values. It was a thousand tiny decisions, each seemingly insignificant at the time. By the time I realized the path I was on, it felt impossible to turn back."

His story revealed something profound about ethical leadership that we don't discuss nearly enough. The most dangerous ethical challenges aren't the dramatic, obvious moral dilemmas—they are the subtle, incremental shifts that occur when we're focused on other matters.

The scenarios in this book draw from well-documented business cases that made headlines and transformed organizations. I have altered names, industries, and specific details, but the core ethical dilemmas represent real situations that leaders encounter every day.

These stories illustrate how principles from an ancient text can illuminate paths through our most modern challenges. What makes Daniel's ancient example so compelling is that he wasn't merely a moral exemplar who avoided wrongdoing. He was a highly effective leader who achieved extraordinary influence because of his ethical clarity, not despite it.

Consider your own leadership journey for a moment. Have you ever felt caught between competing pressures? Perhaps organizational expectations pull you one way while your personal values tug in another direction. Or maybe you've witnessed colleagues gradually drift from their principles through a series of small compromises that eventually lead to significant ethical breaches?

These tensions feel distinctly modern, yet they echo the challenges Daniel faced in the courts of Babylon and Persia. Although the specific details differ dramatically, the fundamental dynamics remain consistent across time and cultures.

ENHANCEMENTS IN THE SECOND EDITION

This second edition builds on the foundation of the first and incorporates several significant improvements:

- **Expanded case studies** across a broader range of contexts, including healthcare, government, technology, manufacturing, and education, that reflect the wide applicability of Daniel's principles.
- **Additional practical** ethical decision-making tools include frameworks that help you address complex situations in which multiple values appear to conflict.

- **Deeper historical context** to help you appreciate the exceptional nature of Daniel's achievements given the constraints he faced. This isn't just interesting background; it offers crucial insights for modern leaders striving to maintain integrity within challenging systems.
- **More in-depth discussion of ethical resilience**— how we can maintain our moral compass during isolated incidents and consistently throughout a career spanning decades and multiple organizations. Daniel's lifetime of ethical leadership provides valuable insights for sustaining integrity amid changing circumstances and escalating challenges.

AN INVITATION TO ETHICAL LEADERSHIP

As you read this book, I invite you to approach it not merely as an intellectual exercise but as a conversation about applying these principles within your own leadership context. What ethical challenges do you face? Where do you feel pressured to compromise? How might Daniel's example illuminate a path forward that upholds both integrity and effectiveness?

The organizational structures we encounter today would bewilder Daniel. Our global supply chains, digital technologies, and complex regulatory environments would be unrecognizable to him. However, the fundamental tensions between integrity and expediency, moral courage and political survival, and short-term pressures and long-term values would feel surprisingly familiar.

I hope this book serves as a trusted companion as you face your own ethical crossroads. When you encounter that moment when the easier choice promises quick advancement,

I hope you'll find in these pages the wisdom and courage to choose the more challenging yet more rewarding path of principled leadership.

Because here's what that fallen executive taught me during our difficult conversation: the trajectory of our leadership is determined not by our responses to obvious moral crises but by the patterns we establish in everyday decisions. Daniel's extraordinary ethical strength wasn't born in the lions' den; it was cultivated through countless smaller choices that prepared him for that defining moment.

Your defining moment may not involve hungry lions, but it will require the same clarity of conviction and practical wisdom that Daniel demonstrated. I sincerely hope this book helps you develop both, so your leadership legacy becomes one of integrity that transforms not only your own career but also the organizations and communities you serve.

With appreciation for your dedication to ethical leadership,

Richard French

INTRODUCTION: THE ETHICAL CRUCIBLE OF POWER AND PROFESSION

Picture a sleek corporate boardroom forty floors above downtown. Victoria Blackwood, the newly appointed Chief Financial Officer of Meridian Global, sits among fellow executives, her heart racing despite her calm exterior. The CEO plans to "adjust" certain financial reports before the shareholders' meeting. The implied message stands clear: either fall in line or risk everything she's worked for.

You've likely experienced this too—not necessarily in a boardroom, but in those moments when the right choice and the easy choice pull you in opposite directions. Perhaps you faced pressure to overlook a supplier's questionable practices, push through a product despite safety concerns, or remain silent when speaking up could cost your promotion. These moments define us as leaders. They're also the moments when most leadership books fall short, offering either rigid rules that overlook real-world complexities or flexible ethics that lead to compromise.

That's why I want to introduce you to someone who mastered ethical success in one of history's most challenging environments. His name is Daniel, and his story demonstrates unprecedented achievement amid relentless ethical pressure.

DANIEL'S JOURNEY: AN ETHICAL LEADERSHIP BLUEPRINT

Before we explore specific principles in the chapters ahead, let's understand the remarkable arc of Daniel's story that will unfold throughout this book.

Daniel's ethical journey began when he was taken as a young man from Jerusalem to Babylon around 605 BCE during Nebuchadnezzar's conquest. Selected for his intelligence and potential, he immediately faced pressure to assimilate into Babylonian culture.

The first test came through what might seem a minor matter—food from the king's table that would violate his religious dietary principles. Rather than simply refusing or reluctantly complying, Daniel proposed a creative alternative: a ten-day test comparing those who ate the king's food with those who followed a simpler diet aligned with his principles. This seemingly small stand established a principled yet practical leadership pattern that would serve him throughout his career.

As Daniel's influence grew, he interpreted dreams for Nebuchadnezzar, providing honest insights even when they contained uncomfortable truths about the king's future. His reputation for integrity and wisdom helped him thrive within the Babylonian court while maintaining his principles.

Years later, when King Belshazzar held a feast using sacred vessels from Jerusalem's temple, mysterious writing appeared on the wall that no court advisors could interpret. Daniel alone deciphered it, delivering the unwelcome message that the king's reign was ending. That very night, the Persian army conquered Babylon, but Daniel's integrity preserved his influence across this radical regime change.

Under the new Persian administration of King Darius, Daniel's effectiveness earned him a position as one of three administrators overseeing 120 provinces. His success created jealousy among colleagues, who manipulated the king into establishing a prayer decree specifically designed to trap Daniel between royal law and religious commitment. Facing the lions' den for his continued faithfulness, Daniel's unwavering commitment led to even greater protection for religious practices throughout the empire.

Throughout his decades-long career spanning different kings and empires, Daniel demonstrated consistent principles while adapting to changing circumstances:

- He maintained clear ethical boundaries without unnecessary antagonism
- He spoke truth to power respectfully but unflinchingly
- He created innovative solutions to ethical dilemmas whenever possible
- He demonstrated exceptional competence alongside ethical integrity
- He built relationships of trust that transcended political transitions

This comprehensive ethical approach allowed Daniel to thrive with integrity in environments designed to force compromise.

MODERN LEADERSHIP APPLICATIONS

Consider this: A young professional, uprooted to the world's most powerful nation, rises through the ranks to become one of its highest officials. He serves with distinction across multiple administrations, handles complex political challenges, and emerges uncompromised and increasingly influential. His approach? Not merely maintaining his principles, but using them to create opportunities for impact.

Does this sound impossible in contemporary professional settings? I understand. When Victoria sat in that boardroom, weighing her response to the CEO's suggestion, the idea of maintaining both integrity and career success seemed implausible. But here's what makes Daniel's story so powerful: he showed that principles, when properly applied, don't limit your success—they strengthen it.

Throughout this book, we'll accompany Daniel as he addresses challenges strikingly similar to those we face today:

- Building trust in low-trust environments
- Speaking truth to power without career sacrifice
- Maintaining integrity while others compromise
- Transforming ethical challenges into opportunities for influence
- Creating positive change in flawed systems

We'll also meet modern leaders who've followed similar paths. You'll see how Dr. Katherine Sullivan, a medical researcher at Westbrook Pharmaceuticals, turned her stand for research integrity into breakthrough innovation. You'll learn how Lauren Barrett's commitment to procurement transparency at Meridian Global led to industry-wide reforms and career advancement. These aren't just stories of doing good; they're roadmaps for doing well by doing right.

This journey begins with a simple yet powerful truth: your principles are not obstacles to overcome but foundations to build upon. In the chapters ahead, we will explore practical strategies for:

- Recognizing ethical challenges before they escalate into crises
- Establishing influence based on trust that endures through leadership transitions
- Developing solutions that align conscience with business objectives
- Building resilience for sustained ethical leadership
- Transforming moral authority into organizational influence

As Victoria sat in that boardroom, drawing on these same principles, she discovered what Daniel learned millennia ago: authentic leadership isn't about choosing between ethics and success; it's about using one to achieve the other.

Are you ready to explore this path? To discover how your principles can become your most valuable professional asset? To master the art of succeeding without compromise? Let's begin this journey together. The challenges ahead may be significant, but the opportunities to make a lasting impact through principled leadership are equally substantial.

ONE
INTEGRITY AND POWER: DANIEL'S BLUEPRINT FOR ETHICAL INFLUENCE

The emergency department at Metropolitan Medical Center buzzed with controlled chaos as Dr. Katherine Sullivan completed the intubation of a critically ill elderly woman. The patient had arrived by ambulance thirty minutes earlier, struggling to breathe and with dangerously low oxygen levels. Now stabilized, she would require intensive care monitoring and likely several days of hospitalization.

When Dr. Katherine Sullivan stepped into the emergency department each morning, colleagues knew what to expect: steady focus, principled decisions, and genuine compassion even during chaotic traumas. As the daughter of a rural family doctor, Katherine had seen healthcare at its most personal. Her father made house calls during winter storms, treated patients regardless of their ability to pay, and demonstrated medical ethics in practice daily.

"Dad always said medicine is a covenant, not a business transaction," she often told new residents. This philosophy guided her choice of emergency medicine over more lucrative specialties. In the ER, everyone received care regardless of status or insurance. Her colleagues called her "the balanced one" for her ability to stay grounded during a crisis while keeping a clear perspective on the patients behind the medical charts.

This combination of practical skill and ethical clarity had earned Katherine respect throughout Metropolitan Medical Center. It would also prove essential when facing a new hospital policy that threatened the equality of care she had dedicated her career to protecting.

"Good work, team," Katherine said, stepping back from the bed as the respiratory therapist secured the ventilator. "Let's get her up to ICU."

The charge nurse, Elaine, exchanged glances with the unit secretary. "Dr. Lancaster wants all admissions run through central triage first," she said carefully.

Katherine frowned. "This patient needs an ICU bed now. She doesn't need another layer of assessment."

"It's the new protocol," Elaine replied, her voice lowered. "They're checking insurance and 'resource allocation criteria' before assigning beds."

This was the third time this week that Katherine had encountered this mysterious new "protocol" that had somehow not been discussed in any department meetings. She had heard troubling rumors about patients being redirected to other facilities or experiencing unusual delays in admission, but hadn't connected the dots until now.

"Call up to the ICU directly," Katherine instructed, her voice firm but quiet. "This patient meets all clinical criteria for immediate admission. I'll deal with the administration if they have questions."

Across town in TechCraft's gleaming headquarters, Victoria Caldwell tapped her stylus against a glass conference table, the soft rhythm at odds with the storm brewing within her. Through the floor-to-ceiling windows of the executive board-room, San Francisco's skyline gleamed in the afternoon sun. The view had always calmed her before, but today, it offered no peace.

Victoria had built TechCraft from a startup in her garage to an AI industry leader. The granddaughter of civil rights activists, she combined an engineer's precision with a philosopher's ethical sensitivity. She believed technology should serve humanity's highest aspirations, not exploit vulnerabilities. Her team called her "The Ethical Accelerator" for her ability to advance projects while keeping moral questions central. Now, her hard-won ethical reputation faced its greatest test as market pressures challenged her principles about responsible technology.

"It's a glitch, Victoria. A minor technical issue, not an ethical crisis." Douglas Sterling's voice cut through her thoughts. The silver-haired board member leaned forward, his custom-tailored suit unable to hide his growing impatience. "Every new technology has wrinkles to iron out. We don't halt a launch over wrinkles."

Victoria met his gaze steadily. As the CEO of TechCraft, she had managed countless challenges during the company's rise to become a leader in artificial intelligence. However, this situation was different.

"Douglas, our testing shows that Prometheus consistently displays significant bias against certain demographic groups.

It's also making critical safety recommendations that our team can't explain or predict." She turned to the screen displaying the troubling test results her engineering team had discovered 48 hours earlier. "This isn't a wrinkle. It's a fundamental flaw."

The Prometheus AI system represented three years of development and over two billion dollars in investment. More importantly, it was poised to become the industry standard for autonomous decision-making across healthcare, transportation, and financial services. The launch was scheduled for nine days from now, with contracts already secured with major hospitals, banks, and transportation networks.

Though working in different fields, both leaders faced the same question: How does one maintain integrity when powerful systems push toward compromise? When caught between conscience and pressure, how can one stay true to values while keeping the ability to make a difference?

In moments like these, the ancient example of Daniel provides a blueprint for navigating ethical dilemmas that modern leaders can follow.

In the ancient city of Babylon, a foreign exile named Daniel showed how to keep his integrity amid the pressures of power. From his early test of refusing the king's food to his later high-stakes confrontation interpreting divine judgment, Daniel developed an approach to ethical leadership that turned constraints into opportunities and crises into influence.

Let's travel back to that ancient court to see how Daniel handled two key ethical challenges, seeing principles that still light the path for leaders like Katherine and Victoria centuries later.

When Daniel first arrived in Babylon as a young exile, he immediately faced a defining choice. The king's official had assigned him food and wine from the royal table, a practice that would violate Daniel's religious dietary laws. This was no small matter. The food represented both royal favor and cultural assimilation. Refusing it could be seen as rejecting the king's generosity or even questioning his authority.

Daniel set a pattern that defined his leadership in this seemingly small moment: clarity about non-negotiable boundaries paired with creative problem-solving that respected legitimate authorities.

Rather than simply refusing the food or reluctantly giving in, Daniel proposed an alternative: "Please test your servants for ten days. Give us nothing but vegetables to eat and water to drink. Then compare our appearance with the young men eating the royal food, and treat your servants according to what you see."

Notice what Daniel did here. He acknowledged the official's legitimate concern about their physical well-being. He proposed a solution that would meet the official's responsibilities without compromising his own principles. He also suggested a measurable test that would provide objective evidence rather than merely asserting his position.

This early interaction established several key leadership principles: identifying clear ethical boundaries, developing creative alternatives, and maintaining respectful relationships even amid disagreement. These foundational skills would serve Daniel well when facing far more serious ethical challenges later in his career.

Years later, as an elderly statesman who had served through decades of Babylonian rule, Daniel faced perhaps his most daunting ethical test. The new king, Belshazzar, had thrown an extravagant feast, using sacred vessels looted from Jerusalem's temple in a flagrant display of disrespect. During this banquet, mysterious writing appeared on the wall, terrifying the king and baffling his advisors.

Daniel was summoned to interpret this supernatural message. Unlike the food test of his youth, this situation involved no creative middle ground. The writing spelled doom for Belshazzar and his kingdom, and Daniel had to choose between delivering this unwelcome truth or finding a more politically safe interpretation.

The king offered extraordinary incentives: "If you can read this writing and tell me what it means, you will be clothed in purple and have a gold chain placed around your neck, and you will be made the third highest ruler in the kingdom."

In this key moment, Daniel reveals the mature version of the integrity he first displayed as a young man: "You may keep your gifts for yourself and give your rewards to someone else. Nevertheless, I will read the writing for the king and tell him what it means."

Before interpreting the writing, Daniel delivered a history lesson that the king didn't want to hear, reminding Belshazzar how his predecessor Nebuchadnezzar had learned humility after his pride led to temporary madness. "But you, Belshazzar, his son, have not humbled yourself, though you knew all this. Instead, you have set yourself up against the Lord of heaven."

Only after establishing this context did Daniel interpret the writing: "Mene: God has numbered the days of your reign and brought it to an end. Tekel: You have been weighed on the scales and found wanting. Peres: Your kingdom is divided and given to the Medes and Persians."

The interpretation was direct. Daniel could have softened the message, found diplomatic ambiguity, or declined to interpret altogether. Instead, he spoke truth directly to power, neither disrespectfully nor timidly, but with clarity that left no room for misunderstanding.

What's striking about both these incidents is how Daniel's integrity created opportunities rather than limitations. His creative approach to the food test earned the respect of his supervisors and established a pattern that allowed him to maintain his identity while serving effectively. His honest truth-telling with Belshazzar demonstrated a moral authority that transcended political position, establishing a reputation that would serve him well even after Babylon fell to the Persians that very night.

Let's return to our modern leaders wrestling with their own ethical challenges.

Dr. Katherine Sullivan had just directly admitted a patient against the new "protocol" requiring insurance verification before ICU placement. When Dr. Christopher Lancaster, the hospital's recently appointed Chief Medical Officer, confronted her about bypassing the system, she faced her own moment of ethical clarity.

"My patient needed immediate ICU care," Katherine replied. "She met all clinical criteria."

"That's not your determination to make anymore," Lancaster said. "The hospital is at a critical financial juncture. Every bed assignment has resource implications that need centralized oversight."

Katherine studied him carefully. "What exactly is this new protocol evaluating beyond clinical need?"

Lancaster shifted slightly. "Healthcare is complicated. We must consider multiple factors, including insurance status, long-term care prospects, and overall resource utilization profiles."

The implications suddenly became crystal clear. The hospital was prioritizing patients with good insurance and favorable financial profiles over those with greater clinical needs but worse payment prospects.

"That's not medicine, Chris. That's financial triage masquerading as clinical judgment."

Katherine's medical training had prepared her for split-second clinical decisions, but this situation created a different kind of pressure altogether. The new protocol wasn't simply an administrative inconvenience; it fundamentally reshaped what patient care meant at Metropolitan. She could almost see the invisible line being drawn between the medicine she had sworn to practice and the system now taking shape around her.

Like Daniel interpreting the writing on the wall, Katherine faced a moment where diplomatic ambiguity wasn't an option. The system was fundamentally misaligned with her core medical values; she needed to name that reality.

But Katherine also recognized that simply stating her opposition wouldn't create positive change. Like Daniel proposing an alternative food test, she needed to find a path forward that addressed legitimate concerns while maintaining ethical boundaries.

In the days that followed, Katherine gathered evidence documenting how the new protocol affected patient outcomes. She worked with colleagues to develop alternative approaches that could address financial pressures without compromising care. She built a coalition of healthcare providers committed to both medical ethics and hospital sustainability.

When finally confronting the hospital board with her findings, Katherine didn't just present problems but offered solutions: "I understand the financial pressures we face. But there are ways to address those pressures without compromising our core mission. Here's how we can do both."

Meanwhile, across town at TechCraft, Victoria Caldwell faced her own ethical challenge with the biased AI system scheduled for imminent launch.

"I understand the financial implications," she said finally. "But launching Prometheus now would violate everything Tech-Craft stands for. We'd knowingly deploy a system discriminating against certain groups and making unpredictable safety recommendations. That's not just ethically wrong—it's bad business."

She tapped her tablet, bringing up a new set of slides. "I'm not suggesting we cancel the launch. I'm proposing we delay by 90 days to address these critical issues. Our technical team has identified the root causes and developed a roadmap to fix them."

Douglas Sterling scoffed. "Ninety days might as well be ninety years in this market. Our competitors will eat our lunch."

Victoria met his gaze directly. "And what happens when the first hospital using our AI makes a systematically biased treatment decision? Or when a transportation system opti-mizes safety for some groups at the expense of others? The lawsuits alone would hurt us badly, not to mention the human cost."

Like Daniel before Belshazzar, Victoria spoke truth directly to power, naming the ethical reality that others preferred to ignore. However, like Daniel's food test proposal, she also offered a constructive alternative that addressed legitimate business concerns while maintaining ethical boundaries.

The board approved a 45-day delay accompanied by a transparent communication strategy. The victory felt small, with several administrators remaining skeptical and Douglas's expression suggesting further resistance. But Victoria had created space for a solution that honored both ethics and business needs.

What Katherine and Victoria demonstrate, reflecting Daniel's ancient example, is that ethical leadership when facing power demands both moral clarity and practical solutions. It's about knowing which boundaries can't be crossed while finding creative paths forward whenever possible.

The outcomes of these modern ethical stands mirror Daniel's experience as well. Initially, both leaders faced significant resistance. Katherine was temporarily suspended from her duties. Victoria watched her company's stock drop 18% following the delayed launch announcement.

But in both cases, integrity created opportunities that compromise never would have achieved:

1. **Institution-wide impact.** Katherine's stand eventually led to hospital-wide reforms in patient triage that balanced financial sustainability with ethical care. Victoria's insistence on addressing bias before launch established new standards for responsible AI deployment throughout TechCraft.

2. **Enhanced reputation.** Even amid financial pressures, the hospital's commitment to patient-centered care strengthened community trust. TechCraft's transparent approach to addressing AI bias earned them industry recognition as an ethical leader when competitors faced backlash for similar issues they had concealed.

3. **Personal influence.** Katherine and Victoria found their spheres of influence expanded rather than diminished by their ethical stands. Katherine was invited to join a national task force on ethical resource allocation in healthcare. Victoria became a sought-after speaker on responsible AI development.

4. **Long-term advantage.** What initially appeared as costly ethical stands provided competitive advantages. The hospital's ethical approach qualified it for additional funding sources unavailable to institutions with discriminatory practices. TechCraft's ethical AI framework positioned them as industry leaders when regulations eventually required similar standards.

From these parallel journeys, we can apply several practical principles in our own leadership contexts:

First, clarity about non-negotiable values provides essential boundaries. Daniel knew his dietary laws were non-negotiable. Katherine recognized that patient care based on clinical need was foundational to medical ethics. Victoria understood that knowingly deploying biased AI violated core principles of fairness and safety. This clarity isn't restrictive; it's freeing, allowing us to focus creative energy on solutions within ethical parameters.

Second, creative problem-solving transforms ethical stands from opposition to opportunity. Daniel didn't just refuse the king's food; he proposed a better alternative. Katherine didn't just criticize the hospital's triage system; she developed a more sustainable approach that maintained care standards. Victoria didn't just block the AI launch; she created a roadmap for addressing bias while preserving market position.

Third, respectful truth-telling builds moral authority without unnecessary antagonism. Daniel acknowledged the king's position while delivering the uncomfortable truth. Katherine recognized legitimate financial concerns while refusing to compromise patient care. Victoria understood business pressures while maintaining ethical standards. This balance of respect and conviction creates the possibility of influence rather than mere resistance.

Fourth, ethical leadership often requires accepting short-term costs for long-term integrity. Daniel risked his position by interpreting the writing honestly. Katherine faced suspension for bypassing discriminatory protocols. Victoria weathered stock declines and board pressure for delaying the launch. Yet these temporary setbacks created the conditions for more lasting success and expanded influence.

Finally, integrity creates opportunities that compromise never could. Daniel's principled stands led to increasing influence across multiple regimes. Katherine's ethical leadership positioned her as a trusted voice in healthcare policy. Victoria's commitment to responsible AI established TechCraft as an industry leader when regulations eventually caught up with their ethical standards.

These principles work not because they're idealistic but because they're practical in the most basic sense. They recognize that although integrity may seem costly in the short term, it creates the foundation for lasting success and meaningful impact.

When you face your own ethical challenges amid powerful systems pushing toward compromise, remember Daniel's ancient example and its modern echoes in leaders like Katherine and Victoria. The path of integrity isn't always easy, but it creates possibilities that ethical compromise never could.

The question isn't whether you'll encounter pressure to compromise your principles. When that moment arrives, the question is whether you'll have the moral clarity to identify your non-negotiable values, the creative wisdom to develop constructive alternatives, and the courage to speak truth respectfully but firmly to power.

In that moment, you might discover what Daniel, Katherine, and Victoria all found: ethical leadership isn't about choosing between integrity and influence. It's about using integrity to create a different kind of influence that transforms systems rather than merely succeeding within them.

As we've seen through the experiences of Dr. Katherine Sullivan and Victoria Caldwell, maintaining integrity while facing powerful systems often creates unexpected opportunities for positive influence. Their stories echo Daniel's ancient example of ethical leadership that transforms challenges into possibilities.

But what happens when the challenge isn't just an ethical decision point but systemic corruption? How do leaders maintain their integrity when entire systems seem designed to reward deception? In Chapter 2, we'll explore how Daniel exposed corruption in the Persian administration and how modern professionals can apply his approach to reveal wrongdoing while offering solutions rather than just criticism.

TWO

FACING CORRUPTION HEAD ON

The fluorescent lights of the state procurement office cast harsh shadows across Lauren Barrett's desk as she stared at her computer monitor, her forehead creased in concentration. As a procurement officer for the Department of Transportation, she had reviewed hundreds of government contracts. But something about this particular set of highway maintenance bids didn't add up.

Persistence defined Lauren Barrett. As a procurement officer for the Department of Transportation, she paid meticulous attention to every contract she reviewed—a trait that had marked her character since childhood.

Building on Daniel's example of personal integrity from Chapter 1, we now explore how Daniel exposed systemic corruption—showing how ethical leaders can shine the light on wrongdoing while creating positive change rather than simply pointing out problems.

"My dad was a military logistics officer," she would explain with a smile. "He taught me that details matter because people's lives depend on them." This wasn't hyperbole in her work, where cutting corners in highway maintenance contracts could lead to real public safety risks.

Growing up in a military family that moved frequently had given Lauren two crucial qualities: adaptability and a solid internal compass. When environments changed around her, her values remained steady. This combination made her effective in government contracting, where she moved through complex political waters without getting swept away by currents of expediency.

What set Lauren apart wasn't just her analytical mind but her quiet resolve. "She never raises her voice," a colleague once observed, "but she never backs down either." This steadfastness would prove crucial as she uncovered a pattern of bid-rigging that implicated powerful figures throughout the state procurement system.

"That can't be right," she murmured, scrolling through the documentation again. Everything appeared proper on the surface. Five companies had submitted bids for the $50 million highway resurfacing project. The selection committee chose Pinnacle Construction, whose bid wasn't the lowest but scored highest on the department's "best value" matrix. This was all standard procedure.

But Lauren had noticed something peculiar. Over the past eighteen months, the same four companies kept bidding against each other on major projects, each one winning in what seemed to be a rotating pattern. More oddly, the losing bids were consistently priced slightly higher than the winning ones—almost as if they were designed to lose by a narrow margin.

She pulled up a spreadsheet she had been quietly assembling for weeks, color-coding the bid amounts, contract specifications, and winning companies. The pattern was subtle but unmistakable once you knew what to look for. It had all the hallmarks of bid-rigging—competitors secretly agreeing to take turns winning contracts while maintaining artificially high prices.

If she were right, taxpayers had been systematically overcharged by millions of dollars. Furthermore, this issue wasn't merely about money. Substandard materials and rushed workmanship often accompanied such schemes, potentially risking public safety.

A sharp knock startled her. Lauren quickly minimized her spreadsheet as Maxwell Fitzgerald, her immediate supervisor, strode into her office without waiting for a reply.

"Barrett, there you are." His voice was casual, but his eyes flicked to her computer screen. "Working late again? You know, you don't have to check every decimal point. That's why we have auditors." He laughed, but the sound held no warmth.

"Just being thorough," Lauren replied with a practiced smile. "Something seems off about the Westridge highway project bids."

Maxwell's smile flickered almost imperceptibly. "The Westridge contract? That was finalized weeks ago. Pinnacle's already broken ground."

"I know. I was just comparing their materials estimates with those of similar projects. There are some unusual patterns—"

"Look, Lauren," Maxwell interrupted, perching on the edge of her desk. "You're new to major infrastructure contracts. They're complex. What might look like inconsistencies to you are just industry standards that take years to understand." His tone was patronizing, as if explaining something simple to a child.

Lauren had been in procurement for eight years—hardly a novice. But she maintained a neutral expression. "Maybe you're right. Still, I think we should look more closely at—"

"We're swamped with the new federal projects," Maxwell said. "The last thing we need is to create unnecessary delays by second-guessing closed contracts." He paused, his voice lowering confidentially. "Between us, some of these contractors have close relationships with the governor's office. Rocking the boat won't do your career any favors."

The implied threat hung in the air. Lauren felt a chill run through her that had nothing to do with the aggressive office air conditioning. She was being warned off, which meant there was definitely something to find.

As Maxwell left, closing her office door with a deliberate click, Lauren sat still, her mind racing.

Lauren found herself standing at a professional crossroads where both paths disappeared into fog. One direction carried the scent of career suicide with uncertain outcomes. The other offered apparent safety but required leaving her professional compass behind.

The contract files on her desk seemed heavier than mere paper, each spreadsheet cell and signature line containing hidden stories of how public trust was being quietly bartered away. Every time she closed her eyes, she saw that pattern of bid rotation glowing like a warning signal that she alone could see.

As Lauren weighed her options, she recalled the story of

another person who had faced a similar ethical crossroads centuries earlier...

The grand palace of Persia gleamed with polished marble and gold leaf, a testament to the empire's vast wealth and power. Inside, Daniel moved through the columned halls with quiet purpose; his aging frame remained straight despite decades of service in foreign courts.

Much had changed since his early days as a captive from Jerusalem. Babylon had fallen to the Persians, and now he served under King Darius, who had restructured the vast empire into 120 provinces, each governed by a satrap. Daniel himself had been appointed as one of three administrators overseeing these satraps, a position of tremendous responsibility.

It was a remarkable place for an exile to find himself—a Jew from conquered Jerusalem now helping govern the world's most powerful empire. But the burden of leadership had grown heavier in recent months.

In his systematic review of provincial accounts, Daniel noticed troubling discrepancies. Tax revenues that should have reached the royal treasury consistently fell short. Resources intended for public works mysteriously diminished before projects began. Reports from distant provinces contained identical language, despite describing vastly different regions and situations.

The situation was particularly delicate because the evidence pointed to collusion among many of the king's appointed officials—powerful men with connections throughout the empire. Any accusation would need to be irrefutable. A single misstep could end Daniel's position and potentially endanger the entire Jewish community, whose status remained precarious despite his personal advancement.

So Daniel proceeded carefully and meticulously. Where Lauren had her spreadsheets, Daniel compiled clay tablets and papyrus scrolls, cross-referencing reports and documenting patterns too consistent to be coincidence. He worked mostly at night, aware the palace had eyes and ears everywhere. He confided in no one except his most trusted friends, who had stood with him through previous challenges.

Daniel understood the political landscape intimately. King Darius prioritized the efficient administration of his empire above all else. The corruption was not merely theft—it undermined imperial authority, decreased tax revenue, and potentially fostered rebellion in provinces where resources failed to arrive as promised. This perspective would be crucial to the king.

The moment to act arrived during a private meeting when Darius requested Daniel's assessment of the empire's financial health. Other advisors had painted a rosy picture, but the king had come to value Daniel's unvarnished truth—a reputation built through years of integrity.

"Your Majesty," Daniel said, his voice steady despite the risk, "I've found patterns in the provincial accounts that require your attention."

With measured words, Daniel laid out the evidence he had gathered. He presented not accusations but facts, allowing the king to reach his own conclusions. He focused on the impact on the empire and the king's authority rather than the moral failings of individuals.

Crucially, he came prepared with a solution: a new system of accountability that would make such corruption more difficult without disrupting the empire's operations.

Darius's face darkened as he grasped the implications. "These are serious matters, Daniel. Many powerful people will resist such scrutiny."

"Indeed, Your Majesty," Daniel replied. "That is why I've brought this directly to you alone. The empire's strength depends on its foundations. When those foundations are compromised, everything built upon them becomes unstable."

The king studied Daniel thoughtfully. Other advisors might have used such information for personal gain, eliminating rivals or extracting bribes for silence. However, Darius had come to recognize that Daniel operated on different principles. His loyalty was not self-serving but rooted in something deeper.

"You understand the danger you place yourself in by bringing this forward?" the king asked.

Daniel nodded, his eyes steady. "I do, Your Majesty. But I would be in greater danger before my God if I remained silent while witnessing injustice."

That response captured the essence of Daniel's approach to confronting corruption. He acted not for personal advancement but from a commitment to a higher standard. Yet his method was neither reckless nor self-righteous. He gathered evidence methodically, presented it strategically, and offered practical solutions rather than mere accusations.

What happened next would become another key chapter in Daniel's remarkable journey through exile. The king authorized a comprehensive audit of provincial accounts, implemented Daniel's proposed accountability measures, and elevated him to a higher authority to oversee the reforms.

Seeing their schemes exposed and their influence threatened, the corrupt officials began to plot against Daniel. Their resentment eventually led to the famous incident of the lions' den, where they manipulated the king into creating a law they knew Daniel would violate by praying to his God.

But even that murderous plot ultimately failed. Daniel's approach to confronting corruption—principled yet practical, bold yet wise—preserved and strengthened his position. More importantly, it created systems of greater accountability that benefited the entire empire, including the Jewish community living in exile.

"Have you ever heard the story of Daniel uncovering corruption in the Persian administration?" her grandfather had asked during a formative conversation in Lauren's teens. "It wasn't just about moral courage. It was about gathering evidence, understanding systems, and speaking truth strategically."

Those words from years ago returned to Lauren now as she organized her documentation of bid-rigging patterns. Her grandfather, a career civil servant who had once refused to approve questionable defense contracts, had seen the parallels between ancient integrity and modern ethical challenges.

Lauren turned back to her computer, Daniel's approach crystallizing into a strategy she could apply to her own situation. She wouldn't act rashly, making accusations she couldn't substantiate, nor would she look the other way. Instead, she would follow Daniel's pattern: gather irrefutable evidence, identify the practical impact, and present her findings in a way that offered solutions rather than just exposing problems.

Lauren worked methodically over the next three weeks, primarily during early mornings and late evenings when the office was empty. She compiled bid patterns across numerous contracts, documenting how prices were consistently inflated by 15-20% above reasonable market rates. She identified communication patterns between seemingly competing firms that suggested collusion. Most disturbingly, she found evidence of substandard materials being substituted after contracts were signed, potentially compromising structural integrity.

But Lauren understood that evidence alone would not suffice. She needed to grasp the political landscape. Like Daniel before King Darius, she had to frame the issue in a way that would inspire action from those with the power to enact change.

The state faced a budget shortfall, and the governor called for belt-tightening across all departments. Meanwhile, a transportation safety initiative had become a cornerstone of the administration's agenda after a bridge collapse in a neighboring state made national headlines.

Lauren realized that the bid-rigging scheme wasn't just about money—it threatened public safety and undermined the governor's major policy initiatives.

She also considered the organizational dynamics carefully. Maxwell wasn't her only superior; Rachel Whitman headed the internal audit division and reported directly to the department secretary. Rachel had a reputation for independence and had previously worked in the state attorney general's office. She would understand both the legal implications and the proper channels for addressing corruption.

One Tuesday morning, Lauren requested a private meeting with Rachel, bringing only a single thumb drive containing her most compelling evidence. She made no accusations against specific individuals; instead, she focused on the pattern she had uncovered and its implications for the department and public safety.

"The data shows a coordinated bid-rigging scheme across major infrastructure projects," Lauren explained, walking Rachel through her analysis. "Based on these patterns, taxpayers have been overcharged approximately $35 million over the past two years. But my greater concern is here," she continued, pulling up quality control reports that showed material substitutions and inspection shortcuts.

Rachel examined the evidence closely, her expression revealing nothing. "You understand what you're implying," she said finally. "This would involve multiple companies and potentially people within this department."

"I do," Lauren replied. "That's why I came to you directly instead of filing a general complaint. This needs to be handled carefully."

"Why?" Rachel asked, her gaze sharp. "Why risk your career over this? Many would look the other way."

Lauren thought about Daniel, who had risked far more while in a much more precarious position.

"Because this isn't just about money," she answered. "The safety shortcuts I've documented could literally cost lives. I couldn't live with myself if a bridge failed or a road collapsed because I stayed silent."

Something in Rachel's expression shifted subtly. "You've done thorough work," she acknowledged. "Leave this with me. Don't discuss it with anyone else, including your supervisor.

I'll need a few days to verify independently and consider next steps."

Those few days stretched into two tense weeks. Lauren continued her regular duties, feeling Maxwell's suspicious eyes on her but giving no indication of what she had done. Had she made a mistake in trusting Rachel? Would her evidence be buried or, worse, used against her?

Then came a department-wide email announcing an emergency all-hands meeting. Lauren's stomach tightened as she walked into the large conference room with her colleagues.

The department secretary, Harrison Thorne, stood at the front, flanked by Rachel and two stern-looking individuals Lauren didn't recognize.

"As some of you may have heard," Harrison began without preamble, "we've launched a comprehensive audit of our contracting procedures in partnership with the state attorney general's office." He gestured to the strangers, whom Lauren now realized were investigators. "This review has uncovered irregularities that require immediate attention."

The room erupted in murmurs. Lauren maintained a neutral expression, even as Maxwell shot her a venomous glance from across the room.

What followed was a significant shift in the department. Four officials, including Maxwell, were placed on administrative leave pending an investigation. Contracts with three construction companies were suspended. The governor announced a task force to reform procurement procedures across all state agencies.

Two days later, a secretary escorted Lauren to Harrison Thorne's office, where Rachel was already waiting.

"Ms. Barrett," Harrison began, "I understand we have you to thank for bringing this matter to light."

Lauren glanced at Rachel, who gave her a slight nod.

"I simply noticed patterns that concerned me," Lauren replied carefully.

"What you did took considerable courage," Harrison continued. "But also remarkable skill. Your analysis was more thorough than some of our formal audits."

"We're restructuring the procurement division," Rachel added. "Creating a new compliance team with direct reporting lines to prevent the kind of oversight failures that allowed this to develop."

Harrison leaned forward. "We'd like you to head that team, Ms. Barrett. Your integrity and analytical skills are exactly what we need to rebuild trust in our processes."

Lauren was momentarily speechless. She had risked her career only to be offered an advancement. Like Daniel, who rose to greater influence after exposing corruption, she was presented with an opportunity to create lasting positive change.

The transition was not smooth. There were challenging days of investigation, testimony, and resistance from those committed to the old ways. Some colleagues maintained their distance, uncertain about where new boundaries lay. However, others stepped forward, expressing concerns they had previously been afraid to voice.

Several months later, Lauren sat in her new office, reviewing the draft of a procurement transparency initiative that would be implemented across all state agencies. What had begun as a solitary stand against corruption had blossomed into broader reform. The new procedures had already saved millions in taxpayer money and strengthened safety oversight.

A knock on her door interrupted her thoughts. It was Rachel Whitman.

"The governor's office called," Rachel said with a hint of a smile. "They want to discuss expanding our transparency framework to other states through a national working group. They'd like you to represent us."

As Rachel left, Lauren found herself thinking once again about Daniel. His story didn't conclude with the exposure of corruption either. It was merely one chapter in a lifelong journey of principled leadership. His ethical stance didn't limit his impact —it amplified it.

Lauren was discovering a similar truth in her own context, centuries later, yet following remarkably similar patterns.

The story of Lauren Barrett and her modern-day experience with corruption shares profound parallels with Daniel's ancient example, offering valuable insights into ethical leadership in challenging environments:

First, **corruption builds protective networks**. Both Daniel and Lauren discovered that dishonest practices spread through systems, creating webs of mutual protection. Daniel faced officials throughout the Persian bureaucracy who benefited from the status quo, while Lauren encountered entrenched relationships between contractors and government officials. Addressing corruption requires understanding these systems rather than simply identifying individual bad actors.

Second, **evidence matters**. Daniel didn't rush to make accusations; he methodically documented patterns that could not be easily dismissed. Lauren followed the same approach, building an irrefutable case before speaking up. This thoroughness protected them both and made their concerns impossible to ignore.

Third, **how one presents the truth is as important as the truth itself**. Daniel framed corruption as a threat to the empire's stability and the king's authority—concerns that would resonate with Darius. Lauren highlighted both financial waste and public safety risks, connecting her findings to the administration's priorities. Both understood that motivating positive action requires speaking to others' values and concerns.

Fourth, **offering solutions creates opportunities**. Neither Daniel nor Lauren simply exposed problems; they presented practical ways forward. This transformed them from mere whistleblowers into valuable problem-solvers, opening doors to greater influence rather than closing them.

Finally, and perhaps most importantly, **ethical stands often create unexpected positive effects**. Daniel's exposure of corruption led to reforms that benefited the entire empire, including his fellow exiles. Lauren's actions sparked changes that improved procurement processes across multiple agencies. Both discovered that integrity, far from limiting impact, amplifies it in ways we can rarely predict.

As you navigate your professional landscape, you may encounter situations where systems seem designed to reward deception or where speaking the truth feels professionally dangerous. Remember that effectively facing corruption requires moral courage and strategic wisdom. Ask yourself:

- What evidence would make the reality undeniable?

- Who needs to hear this truth, and what concerns would motivate them to act?
- What solutions could address the underlying problems?
- How might this challenge become an opportunity to create positive, lasting change?

The path won't always be smooth. Daniel's stand eventually led his enemies to plot against him, resulting in his night in the lions' den. Lauren faced suspicion and isolation before vindication arrived. Ethical leadership often involves periods of uncertainty and opposition.

But both their stories remind us of something powerful: corruption, despite its apparent strength, is built on a foundation of deception. Truth, presented with wisdom and supported by evidence, has a way of creating cracks in that foundation. When those cracks appear, systems that seemed immovable suddenly become open to transformation.

Your opportunity to confront corruption might not involve government contracts or imperial treasuries. It could manifest as a culture of deception in your workplace, a pattern of misrepresentation in your industry, or pressure to compromise standards for short-term gain. While the specifics may vary, the principles remain the same: gather evidence, understand systems, present truth strategically, offer solutions, and trust that integrity creates opportunities that compromise never could.

We don't get to choose if ethical challenges will appear in our path, only how faithfully we'll respond to our values when they do.

While corruption often involves clear ethical violations that can be documented and exposed, many professionals face even more complex challenges. What about situations where the entire system seems designed to force compromise?

Lauren's path required courage in revealing wrongdoing, but at least she had solid evidence of clear violations. Some ethical crossroads offer no such clarity, instead presenting what appears to be impossible choices with no good options.

In Chapter 3, we'll shift our focus from exposing corruption to navigating environments actively hostile to our core values. We'll witness how Daniel's friends confronted the ultimate test in Babylon's fiery furnace, choosing potential death over spiritual compromise. Their ancient example will illuminate the modern journey of Morgan Hayes, a sustainability officer facing intense pressure to approve an environmentally devastating project that would benefit her company financially while harming vulnerable communities. Their stories reveal how principled leadership can transform seemingly impossible situations into opportunities for positive change, even when the path forward initially appears blocked from every direction.

THREE
ETHICAL DECISION-MAKING IN A HOSTILE ENVIRONMENT

The wilderness stretched before Morgan Hayes in silent majesty—ancient trees, their roots plunging deep into soil untouched by industrial machinery, a river bending like a silver ribbon through the valley, distant mountains rising blue against the horizon. Morgan could see the entire area slated for Global Energy Ventures' Horizon Project from this ridge. She held the environmental impact report that would determine its fate in her hand. The same report, whose data she now knew had been deliberately altered to conceal devastating ecological consequences.

The wilderness couldn't speak for itself in the GEV boardroom. Neither could the indigenous communities whose generations of history were written in this landscape. But Morgan could speak. The question that had kept her awake for the past three nights remained: At what cost to herself? And would her voice even matter if raised alone?

While the previous chapters addressed maintaining integrity and exposing corruption, this chapter focuses on an even more challenging situation: what to do when the entire environment seems designed to force compromise, as Daniel's friends faced in the fiery furnace. This requires a different kind of ethical courage.

People often misjudged Morgan Hayes upon first meeting her. With her polished appearance and corporate poise, many assumed she was just another ambitious executive who had traded idealism for advancement. Nothing could be further from the truth.

Morgan's path to becoming Chief Sustainability Officer at Global Energy Ventures began in college when a summer internship took her to communities devastated by industrial contamination. "I realized then that real change wouldn't come from outside pressure alone," she often explained to skeptical environmental activists. "Someone needed to transform these companies from within."

This commitment led her to pursue dual master's degrees in environmental science and business administration, developing expertise that corporate leaders couldn't easily dismiss. Her academic credentials were impressive, but it was her field experience—documenting pollution impacts in rural communities and working with affected residents—that gave her work its moral urgency.

What distinguished Morgan wasn't just her technical knowledge but her rare ability to translate between worldviews. She could speak the language of C-suite financial priorities while never losing sight of ecological realities and community impacts. Where others saw irreconcilable differences, Morgan found points of connection. Where standard approaches created deadlocks, she discovered creative pathways that respected multiple perspectives.

"She builds bridges where others see only chasms," a tribal leader once said of her work. This talent for finding common ground where none seemed possible would be tested to its limits when Morgan discovered that environmental data for GEV's flagship project had been deliberately manipulated.

PRESENT: THE BOARDROOM CONFRONTATION

"If everyone has reviewed the materials, we're ready for your final assessment, Morgan."

Bradley Kingston's voice cut through Morgan's thoughts, pulling her back to the gleaming boardroom on the thirty-seventh floor of GEV headquarters. Twelve executives seated around a table of polished sustainable bamboo—the irony wasn't lost on her—all eyes focused expectantly on her presentation.

As Chief Sustainability Officer, her signature on the environmental impact assessment was the final hurdle before the board would greenlight the $4.2 billion Horizon Project, the cornerstone of GEV's five-year growth strategy. The project would increase shareholder value by an estimated 18% while decimating one of the country's last pristine wilderness areas. Her decision would affect thousands of acres of habitat, dozens of species, multiple watersheds, and several indigenous communities whose histories were intertwined with this land.

"Before I present my assessment," Morgan began, her voice steadier than she felt, "I need to address some critical discrepancies in the data."

She tapped her tablet, and a series of graphs appeared on the wall screen. "The original field samples from the Horizon site show contamination levels that exceed federal limits by 340%.

The processed data in the final report shows levels at 60% of those limits."

Another tap. "The biodiversity impact assessment originally documented seventeen endangered species in the area. The final report acknowledges only four."

The silence in the room thickened. Tyler Whitman, Chief Operations Officer and the project's champion, leaned forward with narrowed eyes. His body language shifted from relaxed confidence to tense defensiveness in seconds.

"What exactly are you implying, Morgan?"

"I'm not implying anything, Tyler. I'm stating facts. The environmental data has been deliberately altered to minimize the project's impact. I've retrieved the original field reports and compared them with what's in our final assessment. They don't match."

CEO Bradley Kingston's expression remained carefully neutral. "That's a serious claim. Have you considered that there might be methodological reasons for the differences? Data refinement is part of any scientific process."

"This isn't refinement. It's fabrication." Morgan displayed a comparison of water toxicity measurements from the same location. "No legitimate scientific methodology explains these discrepancies. This goes beyond normal data processing or statistical adjustments. Someone has intentionally modified these findings to tell a completely different story."

Bradley exchanged glances with Allison Parker, the General Counsel. Something unspoken passed between them before he turned back to Morgan.

"I appreciate your thoroughness. Why don't we table this discussion until you've had a chance to review your concerns with our environmental compliance team? We can reconvene next week."

Morgan recognized the tactic: delay, dilute, dismiss. It was the standard corporate response to inconvenient facts—create enough procedural hurdles and time delays that the urgency dissipates, or deadlines force compromise. She had seen it work countless times across multiple companies.

"The board vote is scheduled for tomorrow. If we proceed with this data, we knowingly violate federal environmental regulations and tribal sovereignty rights. More importantly, we make a decision that can't be undone based on information we know to be false. That puts GEV at significant legal, financial, and reputational risk."

Tyler Whitman made no attempt to hide his frustration. "For God's sake, Morgan, do you realize what's at stake here? We've invested three years and millions in pre-development. The entire strategic plan hinges on this project. Our stock price is based on projected revenue that only the Horizon Project can deliver."

"I know exactly what's at stake," Morgan replied, thinking of the wilderness she had stood in just yesterday. "That's why we need to get this right. The question isn't whether the project proceeds, but whether it proceeds honestly, legally, and responsibly."

PAST: THE DISCOVERY

Two weeks earlier, Morgan had been reviewing routine environmental monitoring reports when Samantha Reed, a recently hired environmental scientist, had knocked tentatively on her office door.

"Do you have a minute?" Samantha had asked, clutching a folder with white-knuckled fingers.

"Of course, come in." Morgan had gestured to the chair across from her desk, sensing the younger woman's anxiety. "Is everything alright?"

Samantha had hesitated before sitting, glancing over her shoulder as if to ensure no one was in the hallway. "I found something concerning in the Horizon data. I wasn't sure who to talk to..."

"You came to the right place," Morgan had assured her. "What did you find?"

"I was cross-referencing the final reports with the original field data, and..." Samantha had placed the folder on Morgan's desk, opening it to reveal two sets of data tables. "These don't match. At all. The processed data shows significantly lower contamination levels, reduced biodiversity impact, minimal disruption to water tables..."

Morgan had felt a chill as she compared the numbers. "Have you shown this to anyone else?"

"No. I thought... well, I've only been here four months. I was afraid I might be misunderstanding something." Samantha's voice had dropped to nearly a whisper. "But the differences are too consistent to be errors. Someone has systematically altered these findings. The statistical probability of these variations occurring naturally across all these parameters is virtually zero."

Morgan had nodded slowly. "You did the right thing bringing this to me. I'll look into it personally. In the meantime, don't discuss this with anyone else."

"What do you think it means?" Samantha had asked, the worry plain on her face.

"I don't know yet," Morgan had replied, though she had already begun forming suspicions. "But I promise you, I'll find out."

After Samantha left, Morgan spent hours digging through digital archives, comparing datasets, and tracing the flow of information from field collection to final report. The pattern was undeniable and deliberate. Someone with high-level access had methodically altered critical environmental data to ensure the Horizon Project would clear regulatory hurdles.

She discovered more than just changed numbers. Entire sections of specialist reports had been omitted. Cautionary notes from field scientists had been removed. Photographs documenting sensitive habitats had been replaced with images from less critical areas. It was a comprehensive effort to create an entirely fictional environmental profile.

But who? And how far up did the deception go?

PRESENT: THE PRIVATE WARNING

"Morgan, wait up."

Allison Parker caught up with her as she headed back to her office after the contentious board meeting had adjourned without resolution.

"Let's talk in my office," Allison suggested, guiding Morgan down the hallway with a light touch on her elbow.

Once the door closed behind them, Allison's professional demeanor softened slightly. "We've worked together for three years, so I will be direct. You're walking into a minefield."

"I'm aware of the politics, Allison."

"No, I don't think you are." Allison leaned against her desk. "The Horizon Project isn't just another development. Bradley has personally guaranteed its success to our major investors. Tyler has structured his entire division around it. We're talking about careers, including yours."

"And I'm talking about breaking federal law and destroying a protected ecosystem."

"Look, everyone appreciates your principles. It's why Bradley brought you on board. But there are times when the company needs practical compromises."

Morgan studied Allison, this woman who had once mentored her through corporate politics. "Is that what we're calling data manipulation now? Practical compromises?"

Allison sighed. "Morgan, think carefully about your next move. If you force this issue, I can't protect you. No one can."

"I'm not asking for protection, Allison. I'm doing my job."

"Your job is to help GEV grow responsibly, not to throw a wrench into our flagship project at the eleventh hour."

"My job is to ensure that GEV's sustainability claims have integrity. What good is my signature on an assessment if it's based on fiction? Why have a Chief Sustainability Officer at all if this is what the company expects?"

As Morgan turned to leave, Allison added, "Just so you're fully informed—if the Horizon Project fails to get approval, GEV's stock will drop at least 20%. The board will demand someone's head. It won't be Bradley's or Tyler's."

The threat hung in the air between them.

"Thanks for the clarity," Morgan said before closing the door behind her.

TYLER'S PERSPECTIVE: THE PRAGMATIST

Tyler Whitman poured himself two fingers of scotch from the bottle he kept in his credenza. The boardroom confrontation had shaken him more than he cared to admit.

Morgan Hayes was supposed to be a team player—that's what Bradley had assured him when he'd expressed concerns about hiring an environmental scientist for the executive team.

"She understands business realities," Bradley had said. "She's not some radical environmentalist."

Now, she threatened to derail the most important project in GEV's pipeline—a project Tyler had staked his professional reputation on.

He sipped his scotch, trying to quiet the voice in his head asking uncomfortable questions. Had he known about the data manipulation? Not explicitly. He had made it clear to the environmental compliance team what results the company needed, but he hadn't asked for details on how they would deliver those results.

Plausible deniability. The corporate executive's shield.

But that shield was growing thinner. If Morgan pushed this issue to the board—or worse, to regulators—people would start asking who had pressured the environmental team. The evidence would eventually point to him.

Tyler set down his glass and picked up his phone. "Get me Michael Sullivan on the line," he told his assistant. The environmental consultant who had prepared the original reports needed to be reminded where his company's bread was buttered.

He stared out his window at the city below. Twenty years he'd worked to reach this position, fifteen-hour days, sacrificed weekends, missed his children's birthdays and soccer games. All to climb to this level where he finally had the authority to make decisions that mattered. The Horizon Project was his chance to cement his legacy and secure his position in the C-suite.

Something would have to be done about Morgan Hayes. The project was too big to fail, and Tyler Whitman was too close to his ambitions to let an idealistic sustainability officer stand in his way.

BRADLEY'S PERSPECTIVE: THE CALCULATING CEO

Bradley Kingston stood at his corner office window, gazing at the city skyline as the day faded into dusk. The Horizon Project had been his visionary initiative—the cornerstone of the legacy he intended to leave at GEV—a legacy of transformation from old-school extraction to innovative, forward-thinking energy development.

Of course, the project's environmental footprint would be substantial. He hadn't expected otherwise. But he had expected Morgan to understand the necessary compromises between sustainability ideals and business realities.

He had hired her precisely because she seemed to grasp this balance. Unlike the environmental purists who viewed any development as destruction, Morgan had demonstrated pragmatism in previous projects. She had found creative solutions that allowed GEV to pursue growth while implementing genuine sustainability improvements.

What had changed?

Bradley's phone buzzed. "Your six o'clock is here," his assistant announced.

"Send him in."

Nathan Crawford, the board member who had once been a petroleum engineer, entered the office. He was one of the old guard, with thirty years in the industry and a reputation for straight talk.

"Quite the dramatic board meeting," he said by way of greeting.

"Morgan's concerns are overblown," Bradley replied dismissively. "She's gotten cold feet about making the tough calls that leadership requires."

Nathan raised an eyebrow. "Are they? Or is she finally looking at the real data instead of the sanitized version?"

Bradley studied the older man carefully. "You knew?"

"I suspected. The numbers in the final report were too perfect." Nathan lowered himself into a chair. "Bradley, I've been in this industry for forty years. I've seen companies bury environmental concerns to push projects through. It never ends well."

"The Horizon Project is different. We've incorporated cutting-edge mitigation strategies—"

"Based on manipulated impact assessments," Nathan interrupted. "You can't mitigate what you're pretending doesn't exist."

Bradley felt a flash of irritation. "What exactly are you suggesting?"

"I'm suggesting you listen to your Chief Sustainability Officer. She's trying to save you from a mistake that could cost far more than a delayed project."

"She's trying to impose idealistic environmental standards that would make any major development impossible."

"Is that what you really believe?" Nathan asked, his tone more curious than confrontational. "Because that's not the Morgan Hayes I've observed in board meetings for the past three years. She's always found practical solutions that respect both business needs and environmental realities. If she's raising this alarm, I suggest you take it seriously."

MORGAN'S REFLECTION: THE ETHICAL CROSSROADS

Morgan sat in her office with dimmed lights, the city glittering beyond her window. On her screen, she had drafted three emails:

The first was her formal objection to the Horizon Project's environmental assessment, which would be sent to the entire board. This would create an official record of her concerns but would likely be outvoted, leaving the project to proceed with her objections noted and then ignored.

The second, a letter of resignation, effective immediately. This would preserve her personal integrity but surrender any influence she might have to shape the project or the company's future practices. It was the clean break, the moral high ground, and possibly professional suicide.

The third, a detailed account of her findings, addressed to federal regulators and environmental watchdog organizations. This would almost certainly stop the project but would brand her a whistleblower—respected by some, reviled by others, and considered toxic by most potential employers.

Each option carried consequences. Each represented a different kind of compromise.

She thought about her journey to this position, the years of work and study, the credibility she had built in both corporate and environmental circles. She had joined GEV because she believed change had to come from within. Walking away meant abandoning that principle. Staying silent meant betraying it.

As she contemplated her choices, Morgan's thoughts turned to a story she had learned in childhood. Three men standing alone before a king and an empire, refusing to bow to a golden statue despite the threat of a fiery furnace.

Shadrach, Meshach, and Abednego had faced an either/or choice: compromise their deepest values or face deadly consequences. What impressed her most about their story wasn't just their courage but their complete peace with uncertainty.

"Our God is able to deliver us," they had told the king. "But even if he does not, we will not serve your gods."

They hadn't demanded guarantees of a happy ending, and they hadn't compromised to preserve their influence. Regardless of the outcome, they stood firm on what they knew to be right.

Morgan wondered what that kind of clarity might look like in her situation. The "furnace" she faced wasn't literal, but professional immolation felt like a genuine possibility. Her career, reputation, and financial security hung in the balance.

Yet something else the ancient story had taught her resonated now: Ethical stands were rarely truly solitary. The three men had stood together. And ultimately, a fourth figure had appeared in the flames beside them.

Was it possible she wasn't as alone as she felt in this moment?

Morgan reached for her phone.

THE UNEXPECTED ALLIANCE

"I need twenty minutes of your time tomorrow morning," Morgan said when Nathan Crawford answered her call. "Before the board vote."

"Concerning the Horizon Project, I assume?" The board member's voice revealed nothing.

"Yes. I've found evidence that environmental data has been deliberately falsified."

A pause. "That's a serious accusation, Morgan."

"I'm prepared to substantiate it. The question is whether anyone on the board is prepared to listen."

Another pause, longer this time. "My office, 7 AM."

Morgan made a second call, this one to Jordan Williams, her deputy in the Sustainability Department. Jordan had been with GEV longer than Morgan and knew the inner workings of the company's environmental compliance systems better than anyone.

"Jordan, I need you to compile every original field report and lab analysis from the Horizon site. Every water sample, soil test, biodiversity survey—all of it. Original source material only."

"That's... hundreds of documents," Jordan said hesitantly.

"I know. And I need it all by 6 AM tomorrow."

"Morgan, what's happening?"

She considered how much to share. Jordan had a family and a mortgage. Involving him could put his career at risk too.

"I'm doing my job, Jordan. Nothing more, nothing less."

"This is about the data discrepancies, isn't it? I've noticed things didn't add up in the final reports, but I assumed there were explanations."

Morgan hesitated. "You saw it too?"

"It was hard to miss if you knew what to look for," Jordan said quietly. "I just... didn't know what to do about it."

"Now you do. Get me those documents, and make copies. Keep one set secure, offsite."

Her final call was to Ryan Thompson, the Indigenous Affairs Liaison. Ryan had been pushing for months to have meaningful consultation with the tribal council whose ancestral lands would be affected by the Horizon Project, only to be repeatedly sidelined by Tyler's team.

"Ryan, does your offer to arrange a meeting with the tribal council still stand?"

"Absolutely," Ryan replied, surprise evident in his voice. "But I thought Tyler made it clear that consultation was—"

"I'm not asking for Tyler's permission. This needs to happen, and it needs to happen now."

"You're going against Tyler? That's career suicide, Morgan."

"Maybe. Or maybe it's just doing the right thing. Can you make it happen?"

"I already have a proposal from the council outlining their concerns and suggested modifications to the project. I can have it on your desk first thing tomorrow."

"Better yet, can you bring representatives to the board meeting at 9 AM?"

A long pause. "That's... unprecedented."

"So is falsifying environmental data."

THE MORNING OF DECISION

Morgan arrived at the office at 5:30 AM, giving her time to review the materials Jordan had compiled overnight. The evidence was even more damning than she had initially realized. Not only had data been altered, but entire studies had been omitted from the final assessment, including a hydrogeological analysis showing that the project would likely contaminate groundwater critical to surrounding communities.

The manipulation wasn't the work of a single person. It was too comprehensive, spanning too many specialized areas. This had been a coordinated effort involving multiple departments, which meant that the directive had come from someone with significant authority.

At precisely 7 AM, she knocked on Nathan Crawford's office door.

The board member wasn't alone. Samantha Reed, the environmental scientist who had first alerted Morgan to the discrepancies, sat nervously in one of the visitor chairs.

"Samantha has been helping me understand the technical aspects of the data concerns," Nathan explained. "Her expertise has been invaluable."

Morgan felt a surge of hope. "You've been looking into this independently?"

"Since the acquisition phase began," Nathan confirmed. "The numbers never added up, but I couldn't pinpoint why until Samantha approached me last week."

Morgan turned to the young scientist. "You went to Nathan after coming to me?"

Samantha nodded. "I was scared. After I talked to you, someone accessed my computer remotely. Files disappeared. I thought..." She glanced at Nathan. "I thought I might need board-level protection."

"Smart move," Morgan acknowledged. "So where do we stand?"

Nathan's expression was grave. "We have ninety minutes before the board vote. I've convinced three other board members to review your evidence, but we need irrefutable proof and a viable alternative. Otherwise, financial considerations will override ethical ones."

"I have the proof." Morgan gestured to the materials she'd brought. "And I believe I have an alternative as well."

THE BOARDROOM: FINAL CONFRONTATION

When Morgan entered the boardroom for the 9 AM vote, she felt a strange calm. The room was more crowded than usual—Nathan had managed to bring in the three board members he'd mentioned, and Morgan had invited Jordan, Samantha, and Ryan Thompson, who arrived with an unexpected guest: Olivia Warren, the local environmental activist who had opposed the project from the beginning.

Bradley's expression darkened when he saw the assembled group. "This is a closed board meeting. What is the meaning of this, Morgan?"

"These individuals are critical to understanding both the problem and the solution I'm proposing," Morgan replied. "I believe the board bylaws allow executives to bring relevant subject matter experts to voting sessions."

Bradley glanced at Allison, who gave a reluctant nod. Legal grounds existed, even if this violated unwritten protocol.

"You have ten minutes," Bradley said tersely.

Morgan began by laying out the evidence of data manipulation, not with accusations but with side-by-side comparisons that spoke for themselves. Jordan distributed tablets containing the complete documentation to each board member.

"This isn't just an ethical issue," Morgan explained. "It's a material business risk. If we proceed based on falsified data, we expose GEV to regulatory penalties, shareholder lawsuits, and catastrophic reputational damage."

Tyler Whitman interrupted. "This is purely speculative. The compliance team has assured me—"

"I'm not finished, Tyler." Morgan's voice carried an authority that silenced him. "The question isn't whether the Horizon Project, as currently designed, violates environmental regulations. The evidence makes that indisputable. The question is whether an alternative exists that serves GEV's strategic goals while complying with the letter and spirit of environmental law."

She nodded to Ryan Thompson, who stood.

"The tribal council has proposed an alternative development approach." He outlined a modified project scope that would protect critical watersheds and cultural sites while still allowing GEV access to significant resources.

Next, Olivia Warren presented surprising research from her environmental organization.

"Our studies show that a scaled-back project focused on these areas"—she highlighted sections of the map—"would yield better ROI over a ten-year horizon due to reduced remediation costs and regulatory compliance issues."

Bradley leaned forward, skepticism written across his face. "You expect us to believe that an environmental activist group is concerned about our ROI?"

"We're concerned about finding solutions that work for all stakeholders," Olivia replied evenly. "Contrary to what you might believe, most of us aren't anti-development. We're anti-destruction."

Nathan Crawford spoke up. "I've reviewed these alternative proposals. They're sound. More importantly, they're honest. I move that we table the vote on the current Horizon Project and direct the executive team to develop a revised proposal based on these alternatives."

The board chairman looked around the table. "Do I have a second?"

The room held its breath.

"Second," said a voice from the end of the table. To Morgan's shock, it was Allison Parker. The General Counsel met Morgan's startled gaze with the faintest nod of acknowledgment.

THE AFTERMATH: THREE MONTHS LATER

Morgan stood again at the ridge overlooking the valley, but she wasn't alone this time. Bradley Kingston stood beside her, surveying the revised project boundaries marked with biodegradable flags.

"It's still a significant development," Morgan observed. "But one that can coexist with this ecosystem rather than destroying it."

Bradley nodded thoughtfully. "The board was impressed with how you handled this, Morgan. Standing your ground without burning bridges. Finding an alternative rather than simply opposing the project." He turned to face her. "That kind of leadership is rare."

"To be honest, I wasn't thinking about leadership," Morgan admitted. "I was just trying to do what was right."

"Sometimes that's exactly what leadership is," Bradley replied. "The share price took a hit when we announced the project revision, but it's already recovering. And the partnership with the tribal council has opened doors we didn't anticipate."

What Bradley didn't mention—and didn't need to—was the aftermath of the board meeting. The environmental compliance team had been disbanded and restructured from the ground up. Tyler Whitman had been reassigned to a lower-profile division. An independent audit of all GEV projects had been initiated.

These changes hadn't come without a cost. Morgan had spent weeks being deposed by GEV's legal team as they assessed the company's exposure. She endured icy interactions with executives whose projects now faced heightened scrutiny. Her year-end bonus would undoubtedly reflect the temporary stock price impact.

But as she looked out over the valley, the ancient trees that would now remain standing, the river that would continue to run clean, she felt a certainty that transcended professional calculations.

"You know what this experience reminded me of?" she said. "An ancient story about three men who refused to bow to a gold statue, even when threatened with a fiery furnace."

Bradley raised an eyebrow. "Religious references, Morgan? That's new."

She smiled. "Not religious so much as instructive. They were willing to accept their stand's consequences, without guaranteeing a positive outcome. That's what ethical courage looks like."

"And did they survive this furnace?" Bradley asked, curious despite himself.

"They did. But the story says they weren't alone in the fire." Morgan turned back toward the valley. "I think that's the part that matters most. You're never really standing alone when you stand for what's right."

As they walked back toward the vehicles, Morgan reflected on the unexpected allies who had emerged during her ethical crisis—some from surprising quarters: Nathan, who had been conducting his own investigation; Samantha, who had shown remarkable courage as a new employee; Ryan, who had bridged worlds by bringing in the tribal council; and even Allison, who had seconded the motion despite her earlier warnings.

The wilderness would remain, not untouched, but unbroken in its essential character. The indigenous communities would have a voice in the development that affected their ancestral lands. And Global Energy Ventures would still meet its strategic objectives, albeit through a more conscientious approach.

It was not a perfect outcome, perhaps, but one that honored the highest loyalties while acknowledging the complex realities of modern corporate life. It demonstrated how ethical leadership could transform seemingly hostile environments into opportunities for something better to emerge.

Morgan thought again of those three ancient figures, standing firm amid the pressures of an empire. Their story had traveled across millennia to provide a template for moral courage in her moment of decision. Her story, in its own small way, would also travel forward, offering guidance to others facing their own ethical crucibles.

ETHICAL LEADERSHIP PRINCIPLES

While Chapter 1 showed how to maintain personal integrity and Chapter 2 revealed how to expose corruption, these principles for facing hostile environments provide a third crucial element of Daniel's blueprint for ethical leadership:

First, **ethical leadership requires clarity about non-negotiable boundaries**. Like Shadrach, Meshach, and Abednego, who knew precisely where they would not compromise, Morgan identified data integrity and environmental protection as values she wouldn't sacrifice. This clarity provided a foundation for all her subsequent decisions.

Second, **ethical challenges are rarely overcome in isolation**. While Morgan initially felt alone, she discovered allies across unexpected boundaries—from board members to activists, from junior employees to indigenous communities. Ethical leadership often creates partnerships that transcend traditional divides.

Third, **constructive alternatives transform opposition into opportunity**. Rather than simply saying no to the problematic project, Morgan and her allies developed a viable alternative that served multiple stakeholders. This approach made ethical leadership a creative rather than merely restrictive force.

Fourth, **courage and wisdom must work together**. Morgan demonstrated courage in confronting manipulation and wisdom in framing the issue as a business risk rather than merely a moral concern. This balanced approach made her ethical stand more effective than righteous indignation alone could have achieved.

Finally, **ethical leadership creates ripple effects beyond the immediate situation**. Morgan's stand led to systemic changes within GEV, including new compliance protocols, leadership shifts, and relationships with previously marginalized stakeholders. Like the three ancient figures whose witness transformed an empire's religious policy, her courage created an impact that extended far beyond the specific project.

When you face your own ethical crucible, remember that the choice isn't always between compromise and career suicide. Sometimes, like Morgan Hayes, you can find a path that honors both integrity and practical realities, particularly when you recognize that ethical leadership is never truly a solitary endeavor.

Morgan had entered what appeared to be a hostile environment designed to force compromise. Yet through clarity, courage, and creative problem-solving, she had helped transform that environment into something better than anyone had initially imagined possible.

In doing so, she demonstrated the enduring truth that Daniel and his friends discovered millennia earlier: ethical leadership isn't about choosing between principles and impact, but about moral courage that transforms hostile environments in ways that surrender never could.

While Morgan faced a hostile environment that tried to force compromise, sometimes the pressure comes directly from authority figures demanding we cross clear ethical lines. In Chapter 4, we'll examine how Daniel handled direct pressure from King Darius in the prayer decree and how modern leaders can maintain integrity when authority directly demands ethical concessions.

FOUR

STANDING FIRM WHEN POWER DEMANDS COMPROMISE

"*I f we are thrown into the blazing furnace, the God we serve is able to deliver us from it... But even if he does not, we want you to know, Your Majesty, that we will not serve your gods or worship the image of gold you have set up.*" — Daniel 3:17-18

The opulent halls of the Persian royal court bustled with activity as Daniel made his way through with purposeful steps. Though his body showed signs of age, he carried himself with the dignity earned through decades of faithful service. His journey had been remarkable—from captive exile to trusted advisor in the world's greatest empire.

The political landscape had shifted dramatically since his early days; Babylon had fallen to Cyrus the Great. Now, King Darius had reorganized the Persian dominion into 120 satrapies for more efficient governance.

The executive conference room in Westbrook Pharmaceuticals' headquarters tower offered a sweeping view of the city skyline from its perch high above the streets below. Still, Dr. Nathan Reynolds' gaze was fixed on the data displayed on his tablet. As

Chief Medical Officer, he had reviewed countless clinical trial results during his career, but these findings sent a chill down his spine despite the warmth of the morning sun streaming through the floor-to-ceiling windows.

The corridors of Westbrook Pharmaceuticals had witnessed fifteen years of Dr. Nathan Reynolds' purposeful stride. With salt-and-pepper hair framing keen eyes that missed little, Nathan combined scientific precision with genuine compassion for patients in a way that set him apart from many of his colleagues in the pharmaceutical industry.

"My father battled a neurological disease for twenty years," he would share with new research teams. "Every medication advance gave us another season with him." This personal connection to patient outcomes shaped his approach to drug development, creating an unusual blend of scientific passion and ethical vigilance.

Nathan hadn't initially planned a career in pharmaceuticals. After fifteen successful years in academic medicine, he was drawn to Westbrook by the promise of developing treatments that could help patients like his father. Growing up with parents who were both educators had instilled in him the belief that knowledge carried responsibility, a principle that guided him through countless difficult decisions.

This deeply rooted sense of purpose would soon face its greatest test when safety signals emerged in Westbrook's flagship Alzheimer's drug, creating tension between scientific integrity and enormous financial pressure.

Where earlier chapters explored various challenges to ethical leadership, this chapter specifically examines how to stand firm when direct authority figures demand moral compromise —as Daniel faced with the prayer decree. This requires clarity

about which lines cannot be crossed, regardless of consequences.

WHEN POWER DEMANDS COMPROMISE: A CLEAR ETHICAL LINE

The data on his screen revealed a troubling pattern in Neuroceptin's latest trial results. The company's flagship drug for
early-onset Alzheimer's disease showed promising cognitive
benefits. Still, a deeper analysis had uncovered a potential
safety signal—cardiac irregularities in a small but concerning
number of patients.

"This can't be happening now," Nathan muttered, rubbing his
temples.

The timing couldn't be worse. Westbrook was six months from
filing for FDA approval and in final discussions with investors
for the funding round needed to support commercial launch.
Any delay could threaten the company's stability and the jobs
of hundreds of employees who had poured years into Neuroceptin's development.

A knock at the door interrupted his thoughts. Rebecca
Matthews, Westbrook's CEO, entered with her characteristic
purposeful stride. Tall and impeccably dressed in a tailored
suit, she radiated the confidence that had propelled her
through the notoriously competitive pharmaceutical industry
ranks.

"Nathan, I thought I might find you here," she said, settling
into a chair across from him. "Sophia told me about the cardiac
findings. How serious is it?"

Nathan appreciated Rebecca's direct approach. Unlike some
executives who avoided unpleasant realities, she tackled chal-

lenges head-on. They had developed a productive working relationship over the past three years, though their priorities sometimes diverged.

"The signal is subtle but concerning," Nathan replied, turning his tablet toward her. "Seven patients in the high-dose group experienced atrial fibrillation. The rate is three times higher than expected in this population."

Rebecca studied the data, her expression thoughtful. "Could it be coincidental? Seven cases isn't a large number."

"It's possible, but I don't think we can dismiss it," Nathan said. "The pattern appears dose-dependent, which suggests causality."

Rebecca leaned back, considering the implications. "What are you thinking?"

"We need additional analysis focused specifically on cardiac events. And I believe we should disclose this finding to the FDA now, even before we have the complete picture."

With these words, Nathan drew a clear ethical line. This wasn't a complex gray area requiring intricate balancing of competing values. This was about whether to disclose known safety concerns to regulators and patients or to conceal them for business advantage. The binary nature of the choice stood in stark relief: honesty or deception, integrity or compromise.

Rebecca's expression tightened slightly. "You know what's at stake, Nathan. We're weeks away from closing our Series D funding round. The IPO preparations are in full swing. Any hint of a safety concern could derail everything."

"I understand the business implications," Nathan acknowlededged. "But patient safety has to come first."

"Of course it does," Rebecca agreed. "But there's a balance to strike. We have responsibilities to patients, yes, but also to our employees, shareholders, and the thousands of Alzheimer's patients waiting for this treatment."

She paused, choosing her words carefully. "What if we take a middle path? We conduct the additional analysis urgently while proceeding with our regulatory preparations. If the expanded analysis confirms a significant risk, we'll disclose it immediately."

Nathan felt the weight of competing obligations pulling him in opposite directions. Rebecca wasn't suggesting they hide the data permanently, just delay disclosure until they had more information. Was that reasonable scientific caution or dangerous rationalization?

"I know exactly what you're thinking," Rebecca said, interrupting his thoughts. "You're wondering if this is the start of a slippery slope. But consider the real-world impact of our choices. A premature disclosure that later proves unnecessary could kill this program. Is that fair to the patients who might benefit?"

As Rebecca spoke, the door opened again, and Marcus Daniels, Westbrook's Head of Commercial Operations, joined them. With his animated gestures and rapid-fire speech, Marcus created an immediate energy shift in any room he entered.

"I hear we have a hiccup with the Neuroceptin data," he said without preamble. "How bad is it?"

Before Nathan could respond, Rebecca intervened. "We're discussing the appropriate approach to some new safety findings. Nathan's recommending immediate disclosure to the FDA."

Marcus didn't hide his dismay. "That would be disastrous timing. Venterra Pharmaceuticals just announced positive Phase II results for their competing compound. The market's watching us like hawks. Any hint of trouble, and our valuation takes a hit that we can't afford right now."

Nathan felt a flash of irritation at Marcus's characterization of patient safety as a "hiccup" and his immediate focus on market positioning. Yet he couldn't simply dismiss the commercial perspective. Westbrook's ability to develop future treatments depended on its business viability.

"Look," Marcus continued, pulling up a chair, "I'm not saying we bury this. But science isn't black and white. These findings need interpretation, context. Seven cases could be statistical noise."

"Or it could be the first indication of a serious safety issue," Nathan countered, holding firmly to his ethical boundary. "Remember Veldrix? Baker Pharmaceuticals saw early cardiac signals, dismissed them as insignificant, and pushed forward. Three years later, they faced a massive recall and lawsuits after patients suffered serious heart damage."

Marcus waved his hand dismissively. "Completely different situation. Their signal was much stronger, and they had other red flags they ignored."

The debate continued as they cycled through arguments about scientific responsibility, business realities, and regulatory strategy. Nathan found himself increasingly uncomfortable with the direction of the conversation. What had begun as a discussion about timing and process was subtly shifting toward minimizing the significance of the safety signal itself.

After Marcus left for another meeting, Rebecca remained. Her tone softened. "Nathan, I know this is difficult. No one is asking you to compromise your scientific integrity. We're just talking about process and timing."

"The line between appropriate caution and inappropriate delay can be very thin," Nathan observed, standing firm on his boundary.

"True," Rebecca acknowledged. "But that's why we have you as CMO. Your judgment is what we rely on." She paused. "There's something else to consider. If Neuroceptin doesn't make it to market, what happens to the patients waiting for treatment? Including those like your father?"

The reference to his father sent a jolt through Nathan. Rebecca rarely mentioned his personal connection to their work, knowing it was both a source of motivation and vulnerability for him.

"That's not fair, Rebecca."

"I'm not being manipulative, just realistic," she responded. "Every decision has consequences in multiple directions. Delay could harm patients through a lack of treatment, just as moving forward too quickly could harm them through unforeseen side effects. There's no risk-free path."

WHEN AUTHORITY DEMANDS MORAL COMPROMISE

Having explored how Daniel maintained integrity (Chapter 1), exposed corruption (Chapter 2), and faced hostile environments (Chapter 3), we now see another vital element of his ethical blueprint: standing firm when authority demands compromise.

The pressure Nathan faced paralleled what Daniel encountered in ancient Babylon when King Darius was manipulated into establishing a decree that prohibited anyone from praying to any god or human except the king for thirty days. The punishment for disobedience was being thrown into the lions' den.

This law created an impossible situation for Daniel, whose daily prayer practice was central to his faith and identity. The decree was not merely a religious test; it was a carefully crafted political trap. Daniel's rivals, unable to find any corruption or negligence in his work, devised a situation where his loyalty to the king directly conflicted with his deeper commitments.

When Daniel learned of the decree, he faced a profound choice: to compromise his prayer practice temporarily and maintain his position of influence, or to uphold his integrity at a potentially devastating cost.

Scripture tells us his response: "When Daniel learned that the decree had been published, he went home to his upstairs room where the windows opened toward Jerusalem. Three times a day he got down on his knees and prayed, giving thanks to his God, just as he had done before."

What's striking about Daniel's response is that he didn't create a public spectacle of his defiance, nor did he confront the king angrily regarding the manipulation behind the decree. He continued his established practice, accepting the possible consequences. His commitment to integrity wasn't about gaining advantage or making a political statement; it stemmed from his understanding of his highest loyalty.

Nathan reflected on Daniel's example and recognized that his situation at Westbrook involved a similar tension between organizational loyalty and deeper commitments. Like Daniel, he occupied a position of significant influence that allowed him to affect policies impacting many lives. And like Daniel, maintaining that influence required moving through complex political waters without compromising his core principles.

The next morning, Nathan requested a meeting with the full executive committee. As he prepared his presentation, he carefully considered how to address this ethical challenge with both principle and wisdom. Like Daniel, who honored the king's position even while disobeying the prayer decree, Nathan wanted to respect Westbrook's legitimate business concerns while maintaining his commitment to patient safety and scientific integrity.

STANDING FIRM WHILE RESPECTING AUTHORITY

William Watkins, a board member with a background in both medicine and business, arrived early for the meeting. "I heard about the Neuroceptin situation," he said, settling into a chair across from Nathan. "Tough spot."

"What would you do?" Nathan asked, curious about William's perspective, given his dual expertise.

William simply replied, "I'd remember why I became a doctor in the first place. Business considerations matter, but some lines shouldn't be crossed, even temporarily."

The executive committee meeting began with Rebecca establishing the context and Marcus outlining the commercial implications of various approaches. When it was Nathan's turn, he took a deep breath and began.

"I appreciate the complex considerations we're facing," he said, acknowledging the business realities. "I've thought carefully about the proposal to conduct additional analysis before disclosure, and I understand the reasoning behind it."

He paused, looking at each person around the table. "However, I cannot support this approach. Our regulatory commitment and scientific integrity require transparency, even when the findings are preliminary and potentially inconvenient. More importantly, our responsibility to patients demands that we err on the side of caution with safety signals."

The room became tense. Rebecca's expression remained neutral, but Nathan sensed her disappointment.

"That said," he continued, "I believe we can address both our ethical obligations and business concerns through a more subtle approach than immediate, broad disclosure."

He outlined a proposal: they would notify the FDA about the finding within 48 hours while simultaneously launching an accelerated cardiac assessment of all trial participants. They would provide context that appropriately characterized the preliminary nature of the finding while meeting their disclosure obligations. They would also develop a transparent communication plan for investors that demonstrated their commitment to both thorough science and responsible development.

"This approach may still impact our timeline," Nathan acknowledged. "But it preserves our integrity, protects patients, and demonstrates to regulators and investors that Westbrook stands behind its science even when it's difficult. Long-term, I believe that builds more value than short-term expediency."

The discussion that followed was heated at times. Marcus argued forcefully against what he called "unnecessary self-sabotage." Others expressed concerns about investor reactions and competitive positioning. William Watkins spoke up in support of Nathan's position, lending the weight of his board influence to the debate.

Rebecca considered all perspectives before making her decision. "We'll proceed with Nathan's approach," she announced finally. "Notify the FDA, accelerate the cardiac assessments, and develop the investor communication plan. This may create short-term challenges, but Nathan's right about the long-term implications of our choices in this moment."

As the meeting concluded, Rebecca asked Nathan to stay behind. "That wasn't easy," she said once they were alone. "For either of us."

"No," Nathan agreed. "But I believe it's the right path forward."

"I do too," Rebecca surprised him by saying. "I needed to test your conviction, Nathan. In my position, I have to consider all perspectives and challenge assumptions. A CMO who folds under pressure isn't one I can trust when even harder decisions come."

Nathan realized that what he had perceived as pressure to compromise had been, at least partly, a test of his ethical boundaries. "Not a very comfortable test," he observed with a wry smile.

"Leadership rarely is comfortable," Rebecca replied. "Daniel wasn't comfortable in the lions' den either."

At Nathan's surprised expression, she added, "I grew up with those stories too, Nathan. They still have something to teach us."

THE COURAGE TO MAINTAIN NON-NEGOTIABLE BOUNDARIES

In the weeks that followed, Nathan's approach proved its value. The accelerated cardiac assessment identified additional cases of atrial fibrillation, confirming that the safety signal was real. The agency viewed their transparency favorably because they had already notified the FDA and begun implementing increased cardiac monitoring.

The investor communication highlighted Westbrook's commitment to thorough science and patient safety, receiving a more positive reception than anticipated. The Neuroceptin timeline was delayed by approximately two quarters as they refined the dosing regimen and added cardiac monitoring protocols. The funding round proceeded, though at a slightly lower valuation. Most importantly, the program remained viable while appropriately addressing the safety concerns.

Three months later, Nathan met with Sophia Torres, the Senior Research Director, who had first brought the cardiac signal to his attention. "I was prepared to resign if we had gone the other way," she confided. "Several of us were. But your stand changed something in the culture here. People talk about it."

Nathan hadn't considered the ripple effects his decision might have throughout the organization. Like Daniel, whose unwavering integrity ultimately influenced the policies of the empire itself, his individual stand created an impact beyond the immediate situation.

As he reflected on the experience, Nathan recognized that moral compromise often disguises itself as a reasonable accommodation to reality. The most dangerous ethical slopes are not the obviously steep ones, but those that descend so gradually that each step seems like a minor adjustment rather than a meaningful shift.

His experience paralleled Daniel's in demonstrating that clarity about non-negotiable values, coupled with wisdom in how those values are expressed, creates possibilities that compromise never could.

Years later, Nathan mentored a young pharmacologist facing similar pressures to downplay safety concerns. Over coffee, she asked what had ultimately guided his decision at Westbrook.

"It wasn't just about regulations," Nathan reflected. "It was recognizing that integrity has its own gravity. When you maintain clear ethical boundaries, they pull you toward better scientific outcomes, not just away from tempting shortcuts."

"But weren't you afraid of the consequences?" she pressed.

Nathan smiled. "Of course. But I discovered something unexpected. Speaking truth respectfully but firmly created more trust, not less. My willingness to risk my position expanded my influence. The temporary discomfort of standing firm gave way to deeper relationships built on genuine respect."

As he observed his mentee reflect on these words, Nathan recognized what Daniel had discovered centuries earlier: ethical leadership isn't passed down through policies but through lived example, one conversation, one decision, one person at a time.

STANDING YOUR GROUND: LESSONS IN MAINTAINING INTEGRITY UNDER PRESSURE

The courage to stand firm when faced with direct pressure from authority requires more than good intentions. Both

Daniel and Nathan demonstrate specific principles for maintaining non-negotiable boundaries:

First, **clearly identify your ethical red lines before pressure intensifies**. Nathan's core commitment to patient safety and scientific integrity was established long before the Neuroceptin crisis emerged. Daniel's devotion to prayer was an established pattern, not a sudden decision. Having clarity about your non-negotiable boundaries in advance makes it possible to resist when pressure mounts.

Second, **recognize attempts to obscure binary ethical choices**. Notice how Marcus tried to frame a straightforward issue of disclosure or non-disclosure as a complex scientific judgment call. When authorities pressure you to compromise, they often attempt to reframe clear ethical boundaries as sophisticated judgment calls. Maintaining ethical clarity requires recognizing these efforts to blur the lines.

Third, **respond with respect while holding firm on substance**. Neither Daniel nor Nathan adopted a self-righteous or antagonistic attitude toward authority. Both acknowledged legitimate organizational concerns while refusing to compromise their ethical boundaries. This approach of respectful resistance makes moral stands more effective and sustainable.

Fourth, **offer constructive alternatives whenever possible**. Nathan not only refused the problematic approach; he developed an alternative that addressed legitimate business concerns while upholding ethical boundaries. Daniel didn't organize protests against the prayer decree but instead found a way to maintain his practice without unnecessary provocation.

Finally, accept potential consequences with dignity. Both Daniel and Nathan were willing to accept the possible negative outcomes of their ethical stances. This willingness to bear consequences isn't martyrdom but a recognition that meaningful integrity sometimes requires genuine sacrifice.

As you move through your own professional setting, you will inevitably encounter pressure to compromise your principles for pragmatic gain. The specific contexts will vary widely, from corporate settings to government service, from healthcare to education, but the core dynamic remains remarkably consistent: Will you bend your highest loyalties to accommodate power, or will you maintain your integrity regardless of the potential cost?

In those moments, think about asking yourself:

- What is the true nature of the compromise being requested? Look beyond the reasonable-sounding justifications to recognize where fundamental values are at stake.
- Is this truly a complex ethical dilemma involving competing legitimate values, or is it a binary choice between integrity and compromise disguised as a subtle judgment call?
- What would be the cumulative impact of such compromises over time? Consider how patterns of small adjustments gradually reshape both organizations and individual character.
- Am I prepared to accept the potential consequences of maintaining my principles? Ethical clarity without courage remains merely theoretical.

The path of integrity in the face of power is rarely easy. Daniel spent a night with hungry lions, and Nathan moved through tense confrontations and potential career risks. Maintaining principle when compromise seems expedient often requires genuine sacrifice.

But both stories remind us of something powerful: moral clarity, applied with wisdom and courage, builds trust that ethical compromise cannot achieve. When we uphold our highest values despite pressure from power, we not only preserve our personal integrity but also create space for positive change that benefits many beyond ourselves.

Success in ethical leadership isn't built on avoiding difficult choices, but on creating a foundation strong enough to withstand them.

The courage to maintain clear boundaries when facing direct pressure from authority serves as an essential foundation for ethical leadership. But what about those situations where the right path isn't so clear-cut?

While Nathan faced a black and white choice with a clear ethical line, many professional challenges fall into murkier territory where multiple legitimate values compete for priority.

Chapter 5 will explore how Daniel addressed genuinely complex ethical terrain where no perfect solution existed. Through the story of Adrian Fairfield, a government environmental official caught between economic development and ecological protection, we'll discover how ethical leadership requires both the courage to uphold principles and the wisdom to find creative paths through genuine complexity where competing goods exist and no obvious right answer presents itself.

FIVE

NAVIGATING ETHICAL GRAY AREAS: DANIEL'S WISDOM FOR COMPLEX DECISIONS

The autumn sunlight streamed through the windows of the governor's office as Adrian Fairfield reviewed the environmental impact report on his tablet. The data was clear: the proposed Riverside Development Project would inflict significant ecological damage on an already stressed ecosystem, potentially contaminating the water supply for several low-income communities downstream.

Unlike the clear ethical boundaries that defined cases of outright corruption or deception, Adrian faced a genuinely difficult situation with legitimate values on both sides. Economic development would bring desperately needed jobs to a struggling region, while environmental protection would safeguard water quality for vulnerable communities. Both represented authentic goods that couldn't be fully honored simultaneously.

This issue wasn't about resisting wrong, but discerning the wisest path among competing rights.

The previous chapters addressed situations with relatively clear ethical boundaries—where right and wrong could be discerned, if not easily achieved. This chapter explores the more common reality of competing legitimate values—ethical gray areas where Daniel's wisdom helps us find a path through genuinely difficult choices where no perfect solution exists.

Adrian Fairfield loved solving difficult problems. While others saw impossible tangles of competing interests, Adrian identified intricate puzzles waiting for solutions. This talent made him particularly effective in his role within the governor's environmental policy office, where he regularly translated scientific data into language that resonated with political realities.

"Environmental protection isn't just about the science," he often told graduate students who shadowed him. "It's about helping people see how their interests align with ecological health."

With degrees in both environmental science and public administration, Adrian had spent years establishing himself as a credible bridge between scientific understanding and political feasibility.

What made Adrian truly valuable wasn't just his intellectual versatility; it was his genuine commitment to finding workable solutions. Unlike many of his colleagues, who viewed compromise as weakness, Adrian saw thoughtful negotiation as a strength. He recognized that perfect solutions rarely existed in environmental policy, but that didn't mean meaningful progress was impossible.

This balanced approach earned him respect from industry representatives and environmental advocates alike. It would also become his greatest asset when confronting the ethical difficulties of the Riverside Development Project, which threatened both ecological systems and vulnerable communities.

Yet, the political momentum behind the project seemed unstoppable. The development promised thousands of construction jobs, millions in tax revenue, and revitalization for a struggling part of the state. Governor Caroline Sheffield had made it the centerpiece of her economic agenda, consistently touting its benefits in speeches across the state.

"It's a glitch, Adrian. A minor technical issue, not an ethical crisis," Natalie Donovan said as she appeared in his doorway. As the governor's political director, she was laser-focused on Sheffield's reelection prospects. "The polling on Riverside looks fantastic. Eighty-two percent support in the districts that matter."

Adrian nodded, giving himself a moment before following Natalie to the conference room where senior staff had gathered. Governor Sheffield stood at the head of the table, radiating the confident energy that had made her a rising star in national politics.

"Adrian! Just the man I wanted to see," she called, gesturing him to an empty seat beside her. "I want to announce the final approval for Riverside at next week's economic summit. I need you to prepare the environmental certification by Thursday."

The room buzzed with approval. The summit would attract national media, providing an ideal platform to showcase the governor's economic vision.

"Actually, Governor," Adrian began, measuring his words carefully, "the final environmental assessment raises some serious concerns. The impact on water quality and wildlife habitat is more significant than we initially understood."

The room fell silent. Sheffield's smile dimmed slightly. "What kind of concerns?"

"The development could potentially affect the drinking water of three downstream communities," Adrian explained. "The mitigation measures proposed by the developers don't adequately address the cumulative impact when combined with existing industrial activity in the region."

What made this situation particularly challenging was not a clear right versus wrong choice. Unlike cases where ethical boundaries are black and white, Adrian faced what ethicists call a genuine dilemma—competing values that could not be satisfied simultaneously. The economic benefits were real and would help many people. The environmental risks were also real and could harm vulnerable communities. Both sides could make legitimate ethical arguments for their positions.

A small reproduction of Rembrandt's "Daniel Interpreting the Writing on the Wall" hung in Adrian's office, a gift from a mentor during his graduate studies. His eyes drifted to the painting as he contemplated the competing values in the Riverside Project. The ancient scene of a solitary figure speaking unwelcome truths to power gained fresh relevance. The biblical Daniel addressed ethical difficulties with both principle and wisdom, finding a path forward when no perfect solution existed.

DANIEL'S APPROACH TO ETHICAL COMPLEXITY

The Persian Empire stood as the ancient world's superpower, its administrative reach extending across what had once been numerous independent kingdoms. Within this vast imperial system, Daniel moved with careful consideration, his years of experience evident in his measured approach to court politics.

After the conquest of Babylon, King Darius implemented a comprehensive administrative restructuring, creating a network of 120 provinces with appointed governors. Daniel had been appointed to an elite oversight council in this new political arrangement—one of three administrators tasked with ensuring provincial accountability.

For a man brought to Persia as a captive, this position reflected extraordinary trust from the king. Yet, this elevated status brought its own challenges and responsibilities.

Unlike the prayer decree situation where Daniel faced a clear binary choice between obedience to the king and fidelity to God, his role in Persian governance regularly required addressing difficult tradeoffs between competing legitimate values. When would strict enforcement serve justice, and when might mercy better advance human flourishing? When should imperial interests take precedence over local concerns, and when should they yield? These were not simple questions with obvious answers but difficult dilemmas requiring discernment.

During his methodical review of regional reports and accounts, Daniel began identifying concerning patterns. The numbers didn't align properly—tax revenues showed unexplained shortfalls before reaching the royal treasury. Infrastructure projects received funding that mysteriously diminished before actual construction began. Official correspondence from widely separated regions contained suspiciously identical phrasing and explanations, suggesting coordinated deception instead of independent reporting.

These discoveries put Daniel in a precarious position. The evidence suggested widespread collaboration among influential officials across the empire—men with powerful connections and significant resources to protect themselves. Addressing such corruption would require absolute precision; any accusation without irrefutable evidence could not only destroy Daniel's career but also potentially endanger the already vulnerable Jewish community residing throughout the empire.

Daniel approached this ethical challenge with his characteristic thoroughness. He conducted his investigations discreetly, often examining records during evening hours when the administrative offices were empty. He maintained strict confidentiality, sharing his concerns only with a small circle of trusted colleagues whose integrity had been proven through past challenges.

The political dimensions required careful consideration. Daniel had developed a thorough understanding of imperial priorities and knew King Darius valued administrative effectiveness above all else. Corruption was not merely an ethical abstraction but an immediate threat to imperial stability, reducing the crown's revenues, undermining public works, and potentially fostering regional discontent when promised resources never materialized. This perspective would make the king more receptive to addressing the problem.

Daniel waited for the right moment to present his findings. When Darius requested a private assessment of imperial finances, Daniel saw an opportunity. While other counselors had painted an unrealistically optimistic picture, the king had come to value Daniel's honest assessments—a reputation earned through years of principled service.

"My lord," Daniel began with appropriate respect, "I have noticed certain patterns in our provincial financial systems that warrant your attention."

Daniel presented his evidence with methodical precision, focusing on verifiable facts instead of accusations against specific individuals. He emphasized the systemic impact on imperial governance over moral judgments about individual corruption. Most importantly, he came prepared not only with problems but also with thoughtful solutions—a comprehensive accountability system that would reduce opportunities for financial misconduct while strengthening imperial administration.

This approach reveals several principles for addressing difficult ethical situations. Daniel moved beyond simple right/wrong binaries to consider:

1. The full context, including political realities and potential consequences
2. The competing values at stake—justice, security for his people, loyalty to the king
3. The creative possibilities beyond the obvious options
4. The timing and manner of action that would be most effective
5. Solutions that could address the core issue while minimizing harm

BALANCING COMPETING VALUES IN THE MODERN WORLD

Let's return to Adrian Fairfield, who is facing his own ethical challenge with the Riverside Development. Like Daniel, he isn't confronting a clear moral wrong that requires principled resistance. Instead, he faces genuinely competing values— economic opportunity versus environmental protection, short-term political success versus long-term community well-being—that require discernment and wisdom to address effectively.

Over the next day, Adrian worked meticulously on both documents requested by the governor. He crafted language addressing environmental concerns for the conditional approval while acknowledging the development's economic importance. He included specific, measurable requirements for water quality protection and habitat preservation that would make a difference if implemented.

He also contacted environmental scientists, community advocates from the affected areas, and even representatives from the development company to explore potential solutions. Rather than merely opposing the project, he sought a path to honor both environmental integrity and economic development.

On Thursday morning, Adrian presented both documents to the governor. To his surprise, Natalie Donovan and Senator Hartford were also present.

"Walk us through the differences," Sheffield instructed.

Adrian explained each approach, detailing how conditional approval would protect vulnerable communities while still allowing the project to advance with appropriate safeguards.

Senator Hartford frowned during the presentation. "This conditional approach creates uncertainty for investors," he objected. "It sends the message that our state isn't truly open for business."

"With respect, Senator," Adrian replied, "it sends the message that we develop responsibly. Businesses want regulatory certainty, yes, but they also want protection from future liability. Ignoring these environmental issues now could lead to lawsuits and remediation requirements that would cost far more than addressing them upfront."

The discussion lasted nearly an hour, with political considerations clashing with environmental realities. Finally, Governor Sheffield raised her hand. "I need to make a decision. Adrian, I appreciate your diligence on this issue. While I don't share all your concerns, I recognize the political vulnerability of ignoring them entirely."

She turned to Senator Hartford. "Malcolm, I'm going with the conditional approval. We'll frame it as responsible development that balances economic opportunity with environmental stewardship."

The senator's displeasure was evident, but he nodded stiffly. "I understand the political calculation. But I expect expedited review of the enhanced mitigation measures. This cannot become a backdoor way to kill the project."

"Agreed," the governor replied. "Adrian will personally oversee the review process to ensure it moves quickly while addressing the legitimate concerns."

As the meeting concluded, Adrian felt conflicted. The conditional approval was better than a full certification of inadequate measures, but the pressure to expedite the review created new ethical challenges. Had he made a difference, or merely postponed the moral compromise to a later date?

This ambiguity is precisely what makes ethical gray areas so challenging. Unlike clear moral boundaries, where the right path is evident (if difficult), these situations often leave us wondering whether we have found a creative solution or merely a more palatable compromise.

CREATING INTEGRATIVE SOLUTIONS

Adrian addressed these competing pressures by focusing relentlessly on the science and the well-being of the affected communities. He arranged for representatives from the downstream communities to meet directly with the development team, putting human faces to what might otherwise have remained abstract "environmental justice" concerns.

When the governor announced the conditional approval at the economic summit, she received praise for her balanced approach and criticism from those who favored unrestricted development. However, this careful position resonated with the broader public, who appreciated a leader making thoughtful decisions instead of simplistic pronouncements.

Three months later, the enhanced mitigation plan was finalized. It included state-of-the-art water quality monitoring, expanded wetland preservation areas, and specific protections for the watershed impacting downstream communities. The additional measures increased the project's cost by 4%—significant but not prohibitive.

"You've managed to thread an impossible needle," Governor Sheffield told Adrian when the final plan was approved. "Hartford isn't happy about the delays, but even he admits the project is more defensible now."

"The communities downstream are the real winners," Adrian replied. "They get both the economic benefits and protection for their water supply."

As he left the governor's office, Adrian reflected on the journey from that initial confrontation to the final outcome. His refusal to accept an all-or-nothing choice between the economy and the environment created space for a different approach, not perfect, but significantly better than what would have otherwise happened.

Like Daniel addressing the complex ethical terrain of Persian governance, Adrian upheld his integrity while acknowledging the legitimacy of competing values. And like Daniel, whose dedication to both justice and practical governance led to broader reforms, Adrian's principled approach impacted policy beyond the immediate issue, establishing a new standard for evaluating development projects.

DISCERNMENT IN ETHICAL GRAY AREAS: FINDING WISDOM IN COMPLEXITY

What guidance can we derive from Daniel's example for addressing murky waters where multiple legitimate values compete for priority?

First, genuine ethical dilemmas require deeper analysis than simple right or wrong judgments. Both Daniel and Adrian recognized the complexity of their situations and resisted the temptation to oversimplify. They acknowledged valid competing values instead of entirely dismissing one side. Unlike scenarios that demand unwavering resistance to clear wrongs, these complex situations necessitate discernment to uncover integrative solutions.

Second, effective ethical leadership in gray areas often involves reframing the issue. Daniel recast corruption as a threat to imperial effectiveness rather than merely a moral failing. Adrian repositioned environmental protection as long-term economic security instead of an obstacle to development. This reframing helps identify common ground between seemingly opposing positions and creates space for creative solutions.

Third, solutions to ethical dilemmas often arise from a profound contextual understanding rather than from abstract principles alone. Daniel's thorough knowledge of Persian governance enabled him to propose a new accountability system. Adrian's expertise in both environmental science and economic development allowed him to create conditions that served multiple values. This understanding transforms ethical leadership from theoretical idealism to practical wisdom.

Fourth, timing is crucial in ethical gray areas. Daniel waited for the right moment to present his findings to the king. Adrian developed his alternative approach before the decisive meeting, which enabled him to offer solutions instead of merely raising problems when the moment arrived. Strategic timing often determines whether ethical insights foster positive change or merely generate resistance.

Finally, ethical leadership in complex situations requires follow-through beyond the initial decision. Daniel's exposure of corruption led to systemic reforms. Adrian committed to personally oversee the review process to ensure that environmental protections were not sacrificed for expediency. True ethical leadership is not satisfied with symbolic victories but pursues substantive implementation.

These principles illuminate a path through ethical complexity that honors multiple values while maintaining core integrity. They show us that ethical leadership isn't about rigid absolutes or flexible relativism but about principled creativity that serves genuine human flourishing.

The examples of Daniel addressing corruption in Persia and Adrian addressing complex environmental decisions reveal that gray areas require more than rules or compromise. They demand thoughtful synthesis where moral conviction guides practical action and where wisdom tempers idealism without diminishing it.

This integration of ethical clarity with real-world savvy finds paths that neither rigid absolutism nor easy compromise could discover.

As you address your own ethical gray areas, remember that the most challenging moral questions rarely present themselves as clear choices between right and wrong. More often, they arise as tensions between competing values, each with legitimate claims on our conscience.

In those moments, consider asking yourself:

- What are the multiple values at stake in this situation, and are there ways to honor more than one?
- Am I seeing this as an all-or-nothing choice when there might be creative third options?
- What deeper contextual understanding might reveal solutions not immediately apparent?
- How can I reframe this issue to find common ground between seemingly opposed positions?
- What timing and preparation would make my ethical influence most effective?

The path through ethical gray areas is rarely smooth or straightforward. Daniel faced ongoing resistance from corrupt officials whose schemes he had exposed. Adrian addressed persistent pressure from both economic and environmental interests. Yet both demonstrated that principled leadership does not require rigid absolutism; it demands thoughtful discernment that honors multiple values while maintaining core integrity.

These principles for finding wisdom in ethical gray areas complete the foundational elements of Daniel's blueprint—from integrity (Chapter 1) to exposing corruption (Chapter 2) to surviving hostile environments (Chapter 3) to standing firm against authority (Chapter 4)—giving us a comprehensive approach to ethical leadership across diverse situations.

Your opportunity to demonstrate this kind of ethical leadership may arise in contexts vastly different from ancient Persia or contemporary environmental policy. You may encounter competing priorities in allocating limited resources, balancing transparency with privacy concerns, or weighing short-term gains against long-term sustainability.

In those moments when no perfect solution exists, remember Daniel's wisdom and Adrian's example. The real challenge isn't determining if you'll face ethical dilemmas; it's developing the wisdom to address them when they inevitably arise.

In the next chapter, we will explore another dimension of ethical leadership: addressing competing loyalties. When obligations to organizations clash with professional ethics or personal values, how do we determine which loyalty should prevail? We will see how Daniel maintained appropriate loyalties to earthly authorities while recognizing the higher principles that sometimes required him to take different paths. We will also meet Valerie Brunswick, a corporate counsel facing competing loyalties to her company, the law, and vulnerable communities affected by environmental contamination.

SIX

THE ETHICS OF LOYALTY AND JUSTICE

V alerie Brunswick stared at the environmental impact report on her desk, her legal training immediately recognizing the implications buried in its technical language. As general counsel for Pinnacle Automotive, one of the nation's largest manufacturers, she had reviewed countless documents with potentially significant legal consequences. However, this one felt different.

If you asked Valerie Brunswick about her unusual career path, she would likely flash a wry smile. "I wanted to change the system, so I joined it," she might explain, referencing her journey from environmental activist to corporate attorney. As general counsel for Pinnacle Automotive, Valerie brought a perspective few others in the C-suite shared.

Before law school, Valerie spent five years with an environmental justice organization, witnessing firsthand how industrial pollution disproportionately impacted vulnerable communities. Rather than remaining an outside critic, she deliberately chose corporate law to influence industry practices from within. "Sometimes you need to be in the room where decisions happen," she often reflected.

This dual perspective, as both a former activist and a corporate attorney, gave Valerie an unusual ability to perceive multiple dimensions of ethical challenges. Her colleagues recognized her for her strategic thinking and measured responses rather than for moral grandstanding. She successfully handled numerous complex legal situations by finding solutions that served both corporate interests and broader social responsibilities.

This carefully crafted professional identity would encounter its greatest test when environmental testing uncovered substantial contamination near Pinnacle's flagship manufacturing facility, and evidence indicated that the company had hidden the problem for months.

While previous chapters explored maintaining integrity, exposing corruption, surviving hostile environments, and standing firm against authority, this chapter examines a different ethical challenge: handling competing loyalties. When obligations to organizations conflict with professional ethics or basic human welfare, how do we determine which loyalty should prevail? Daniel's example with the prayer decree shows how to honor multiple obligations while maintaining clarity about which takes ultimate precedence.

The report prepared by the company's environmental compliance team documented chemical contamination in groundwater near its flagship manufacturing facility in Michigan. The levels exceeded regulatory thresholds by a concerning margin. More troubling, internal correspondence attached to the report suggested that mid-level managers had been aware of the issue for nearly eighteen months without notifying the appropriate authorities.

Under federal and state environmental regulations, Pinnacle had a legal obligation to report such contamination within 24 hours of discovery. The eighteen-month delay created serious legal exposure, including the potential for criminal penalties for those responsible. The contamination itself posed health risks to nearby communities that relied on groundwater for drinking water.

Valerie rubbed her temples, feeling the weight of competing obligations. As general counsel, her primary duty was to protect the company's legal interests. As an officer of the court, she had ethical responsibilities to uphold the law. Additionally, as someone who had grown up in a similar industrial community, she couldn't ignore the families potentially consuming contaminated water.

A knock at her door interrupted her thoughts. Vincent Callahan, Pinnacle's CEO, entered without waiting for a response. Tall, confident, and impeccably dressed, he exuded the charismatic authority that had propelled him to the top leadership position two years prior.

"Valerie, I hear you've been asking questions about the Mitchell Plant situation," he said, settling into a chair across from her desk.

She nodded, studying his expression carefully. "The environmental report arrived this morning. We have a serious issue, Vincent."

"How serious?" he asked, his tone measured.

"Federal and state reporting requirements have been violated. The contamination exceeds permissible levels by 380 percent.

And the evidence suggests managers knowingly concealed the problem." She pushed the report across her desk. "We're legally obligated to notify regulators immediately."

Vincent glanced at the report but didn't open it. "What's our exposure if this becomes public?"

"Substantial," Valerie replied. "Regulatory fines will run into the millions. Civil liability from affected residents could be significantly higher. There's also potential criminal liability for whoever conceals the contamination."

"And if we handle this internally? Fix the problem without the regulatory circus?"

The question hung in the air between them. Valerie chose her next words carefully.

"The legal obligation to report isn't optional, Vincent. It's mandatory. The violation has already occurred. The question now is whether we compound it."

Vincent leaned forward. "Look, Valerie, I understand the technical requirements. But I'm talking about practical reality. The Mitchell Plant employs three thousand people in a community with few other opportunities. If regulators swoop in, production could be halted for months. Jobs would be lost. The economic impact would devastate the region."

"And the health impact of contaminated water could devastate families," Valerie countered.

"Which is why we'll fix the contamination issue immediately," Vincent assured her. "I'll authorize whatever resources are needed. But we do it quietly, efficiently, without creating a media frenzy and regulatory nightmare."

His expression softened. "Sometimes loyalty to the greater good requires flexibility on technical compliance."

Valerie felt the full weight of the moment. Vincent wasn't asking her to ignore the problem—he was proposing to address the contamination while avoiding the mandatory reporting requirements. It was a pragmatic approach that would protect jobs and prevent economic hardship in the community. However, it would also violate clear legal obligations and potentially leave affected residents unaware of risks to their water supply.

"I need to think about this," she said finally.

Vincent nodded, rising to leave. "Of course. But don't take too long. Every day increases our exposure."

At the door, he turned back. "Remember, Valerie, thousands of families depend on Pinnacle for their livelihoods. Sometimes loyalty to people has to outweigh loyalty to abstract rules."

As the door closed behind him, Valerie found herself contemplating the nature of true loyalty. To whom did she owe her primary allegiance? The company that employed her? The law she had sworn to uphold? The communities that were potentially drinking contaminated water?

As these questions swirled in her mind, she reflected on another time, another place, where a man faced an even more significant test of competing loyalties...

DANIEL'S TEST OF COMPETING LOYALTIES

The royal palace of Babylon hushed as King Darius signed the decree presented by his administrators and satraps. For thirty days, no one in the empire could pray to any god or human except for the king. Anyone violating this command would face a capital sentence in the royal menagerie, where hungry predators awaited.

The king, flattered by the proposal and focused on the immense task of organizing his newly conquered territories, scarcely noticed the unusual nature of the request. However, the officials who crafted the decree exchanged subtle glances of satisfaction. Their trap was set.

The target of their scheme was Daniel, who had risen to extraordinary influence as one of Darius's top three administrators. His exceptional integrity and wisdom had earned the king's trust, and rumors suggested he would soon be elevated above all other officials in the empire. This prospect alarmed those whose corrupt practices would struggle under Daniel's oversight.

Finding no evidence of wrongdoing in his professional conduct, they devised a plan to create an impossible choice between loyalty to the king and loyalty to his God. They knew that Daniel's daily habit included praying toward Jerusalem three times a day—a practice central to his faith and identity as an exile from Judah.

When Daniel learned of the decree, he faced a difficult dilemma of competing loyalties. As a high government official, he had obligations to respect the king's authority and laws. His position of influence allowed him to protect his fellow Jews and promote justice throughout the empire. Maintaining that influence required political prudence and the avoidance of unnecessary conflict.

Yet Daniel also possessed an unshakeable loyalty to his God—a commitment that defined his identity and guided his every decision. This loyalty was not merely a personal preference; it formed the foundation of his integrity and served as the source of the wisdom that made him valuable to successive kings.

The decree created an irreconcilable conflict. No compromise existed. Either Daniel would continue his prayer practice and violate the king's command, or he would suspend his prayers and betray his fundamental spiritual commitment.

Scripture recounts Daniel's response: "When Daniel learned that the decree had been published, he went home to his upstairs room where the windows opened toward Jerusalem. Three times a day he got down on his knees and prayed, giving thanks to his God, just as he had done before."

Notice what Daniel did not do. He did not publicly protest against the decree, organize resistance among other Jewish exiles, or confront the king about the law's manipulative nature. He simply continued his established practice of faithfulness, fully aware of the consequences.

His enemies, watching his house, immediately reported him to King Darius. Upon suddenly recognizing the trap he had unwittingly authorized, the king felt great distress; he was determined to rescue Daniel and made every effort to save him before sundown. But the law of the Medes and Persians, once signed, could not be revoked—a constitutional safeguard against arbitrary rule that now became a trap for both Daniel and the king who valued him.

With deep regret, Darius ordered Daniel to face his punishment, saying, "May your God, whom you serve continually, rescue you!"

What followed became one of history's most renowned demonstrations of divine protection. Although thrown into mortal danger, Daniel emerged the next morning unharmed, protected by what he described as divine intervention that "shut the lions' mouths." This miraculous preservation led King Darius to issue a decree honoring Daniel's God throughout the empire.

What's remarkable about this story is how Daniel handled competing loyalties without diminishing either one. He maintained genuine respect for the king's authority while refusing to compromise his higher commitment to God. He didn't vilify those who sought his destruction or rail against the injustice of his situation. He accepted the consequences of his choice with dignity and trust.

The outcome—Daniel's miraculous preservation through the night and his eventual vindication—demonstrates something important about competing loyalties: when higher principles are honored at personal cost, unexpected possibilities often emerge. Darius, overjoyed at Daniel's survival, not only restored him to his position but also issued a decree that the God of Daniel should be respected throughout the empire.

Daniel's unwavering commitment to his highest loyalty, embraced with both courage and humility, ultimately created far greater protection for his people than any political compromise could have achieved. His willingness to face death rather than violate his principles led to systemic change that impacted the entire empire.

FINDING CLARITY IN COMPETING LOYALTIES

The Sunday school classroom of Valerie's childhood materialized in her memory with unexpected clarity. Mrs. Abernathy, with her felt board figures, tells Daniel's story to wide-eyed children. "Daniel had to decide what mattered most," she had explained, placing the tiny felt lion beside the kneeling figure.

Valerie had been captivated by the idea that principles could be worth risking everything for. Now, three decades later, as she stared at evidence of groundwater contamination and corporate concealment, that childhood lesson crystallized into adult reality. Some choices truly did reveal what you valued most.

Like Daniel, she needed to determine which loyalty took precedence when conflicts arose. Similarly, she had to find a response that respected all legitimate obligations while clarifying their proper hierarchy.

After several minutes of reflection, Valerie reached for her phone and called Dr. Rebecca Thornton, an environmental scientist with whom she had collaborated on previous compliance issues. Without revealing specific details, she arranged an urgent meeting to discuss "a hypothetical contamination scenario." She needed expert input on the actual health risks before making her decision.

Two hours later, Valerie sat across from Rebecca in a coffee shop several miles from Pinnacle's offices. After securing a commitment of confidentiality, she outlined the situation in detail.

"Based on these contaminant levels," Rebecca said after reviewing the data, "residents using groundwater should be notified immediately. The cancer risk exceeds accepted thresholds by a significant margin. And there are potential developmental risks for children and pregnant women."

"How quickly could remediation address the issue?" Valerie asked.

"Even with aggressive measures, groundwater contamination takes time to resolve. It may take months, potentially years, depending on the extent of the plume. In the meantime, affected residents should use alternative water sources."

This confirmed Valerie's concerns. Vincent's proposal to "fix the problem quietly" couldn't protect community members from ongoing exposure during the remediation process. People needed to understand the risks to make informed decisions about their water usage.

On her drive back to the office, Valerie carefully considered her options. Refusing to cooperate with Vincent's approach might prompt him to exclude her from the process entirely, bringing in outside counsel more willing to prioritize the company's interests above all else. Threatening to report the violation herself would likely end her career at Pinnacle and potentially in corporate law altogether.

She required a response that acknowledged valid business concerns while upholding her highest commitments to justice and professional ethics. Like Daniel before Darius, she needed wisdom to handle conflicting obligations without unnecessary hostility.

When she returned to her office, Valerie drafted a formal legal memorandum for Vincent and the board of directors. The document systematically outlined:

1. Federal and state regulations establish clear legal reporting requirements.
2. The significant penalties for non-compliance, including possible criminal liability.
3. The documented health risks to community members.
4. A proposed comprehensive response plan.

The response plan was where Valerie demonstrated the thoughtfulness that often marks the highest forms of ethical leadership. Rather than presenting an overly simplistic choice between compliance and non-compliance, she outlined a third path that addressed legitimate company concerns while fulfilling legal obligations:

I recommend immediate voluntary disclosure to regulators and a comprehensive remediation plan that exceeds compliance requirements. We should simultaneously announce community support measures, including:

- Free water testing for all residents within the potential exposure area
- Provision of water filtration systems for affected households
- A transparent health monitoring program for concerned residents
- Community investment projects developed in consultation with local leaders

This approach turns a potential crisis into an opportunity to demonstrate corporate responsibility. While the initial costs will be significant, they are overshadowed by the potential liability of non-disclosure. More importantly, this strategy safeguards both community health and the company's long-term interests.

Valerie concluded the memorandum by clearly stating her position: "As general counsel, I cannot support non-disclosure of known environmental violations. Such a course would violate my professional ethical obligations and expose the company to severe legal consequences. I am prepared to work tirelessly to implement the approach outlined above to best serve all stakeholders."

The document acknowledged the company's legitimate concerns about economic impact while maintaining an unwavering commitment to legal compliance and community welfare. Similarly to Daniel's response to the prayer decree, it accepted potential personal costs without unnecessary provocation or self-righteousness.

Valerie sent the memorandum requesting an emergency board meeting. She then waited, knowing that her career at Pinnacle could effectively end once Vincent read her unequivocal position.

To her surprise, the CEO requested a meeting with her before including the entire board. When she entered his office, Vincent's expression was serious but not hostile.

"Your memo makes a compelling case," he said without preamble. "I don't like it, but I respect the clarity of your position."

"I tried to find a path that addresses everyone's legitimate concerns," Valerie replied.

Vincent nodded. "The proactive community support measures are smart. They'd cost less than litigation and generate goodwill."

"They're also the right thing to do for families potentially drinking contaminated water," Valerie added quietly.

Something shifted in Vincent's expression. "You know, I started on the production floor thirty years ago. Worked my way up. Those are my people in Mitchell. I never intended to put them at risk."

He sighed. "I was thinking about the economic impact and the jobs. I should have thought more about the health impact."

"It's not too late to address both," Valerie said.

Vincent studied her for a moment. "Draft the disclosure documents and the community support proposal. I'll present them to the board with my full endorsement."

Over the next several weeks, Pinnacle Automotive implemented the approach Valerie had outlined. The company voluntarily disclosed the contamination to regulators, presented a comprehensive remediation plan, and initiated community support measures that exceeded legal requirements.

The initial response included regulatory penalties, negative press coverage, and a temporary drop in stock price. However, the narrative shifted as the company demonstrated a genuine commitment to resolving the issue and supporting affected residents. Community leaders who had initially been outraged became partners in developing effective solutions.

Five months later, Valerie sat in a town hall meeting in Mitchell, listening as residents discussed the progress of remediation efforts. The company had not only provided alternative water sources but was also funding health monitoring and investing in community development projects that local leaders prioritized.

"You know, we were ready to go to war with Pinnacle when this first came out," one resident told her after the meeting. "But the way you've responded—listening to our concerns, being transparent about the process, actually investing in solutions—it's changed how we see the company."

As Valerie drove back to headquarters, she reflected on how her decision had unfolded. By maintaining her utmost loyalty to justice and professional ethics, even at potential personal cost, she had helped create outcomes that served everyone's best interests: the community received immediate protection and long-term support; the company rebuilt trust and avoided the most severe legal consequences; and she herself gained increased influence within Pinnacle to shape ethical policies going forward.

Like Daniel, whose unwavering commitment to his highest loyalty eventually brought greater protection for his people and respect for his faith throughout the empire, Valerie's principled stance created opportunities that compromise could never achieve.

PRINCIPLES FOR HANDLING COMPETING LOYALTIES

Building on the foundation of integrity (Chapter 1), the courage to expose wrongdoing (Chapter 2), resilience in hostile environments (Chapter 3), firmness when facing authority (Chapter 4), and wisdom in ethical gray areas (Chapter 5), we now add another crucial element to Daniel's blueprint: clarity in competing loyalties.

Like a skilled navigator charting a course through treacherous waters, Valerie discovered essential landmarks for maintaining ethical direction amid competing loyalties.

The first landmark is a proper loyalty hierarchy. Just as navigators distinguish between true and magnetic north, Valerie recognized that not all loyalties carry equal weight. Her obligations to the law and vulnerable communities served as fixed points that could not be sacrificed for organizational expediency.

The second landmark is respectful communication in all directions. Much like a captain who communicates clearly with both officers and crew, Valerie maintained appropriate respect for legitimate concerns at all levels while never compromising her ultimate direction.

The third landmark is solution-oriented thinking. Like charting a course through perilous shoals, her approach uncovered paths that honored multiple values without compromising core principles.

The journey of ethical leadership rarely follows a straight path. However, for those willing to proceed with both courage and wisdom, it leads to destinations that compromise could never reach—places where genuine trust flourishes and lasting value is created.

As you handle challenges in your professional setting, you will inevitably encounter tension between organizational loyalty and commitment to higher principles. The specific contexts will vary widely—from corporate settings to healthcare, from education to public service—but the core dynamic remains remarkably consistent: What do you do when organizational interests conflict with legal requirements, professional ethics, or basic human welfare?

In those moments, consider asking yourself:

- What is the proper hierarchy of my loyalties in this situation? Which commitments should take precedence when they cannot all be satisfied simultaneously?
- How can I honor my highest loyalties while appropriately respecting legitimate organizational concerns?

- Is there an effective third path that could satisfy the essential interests of all stakeholders while upholding ethical boundaries?
- Am I prepared to accept a potential personal cost to uphold my integrity?

Addressing loyalty conflicts is seldom straightforward. Daniel's choice had life-threatening consequences, while Valerie risked her career and professional reputation. Maintaining the highest loyalties often requires true sacrifice and bravery.

But both stories remind us of something important: Clarity about our highest commitments, acted upon with courage and wisdom, creates solutions that ethical confusion never could. When we maintain integrity in loyalty conflicts, we not only preserve our moral compass but also generate unexpected solutions that benefit many beyond ourselves.

Most importantly, remember that true loyalty to organizations is not demonstrated through ethical compromise but through principled actions that serve their legitimate long-term interests. Daniel's faithfulness brought greater stability to the empire than any political accommodation could have achieved. Valerie's ethical stance protected Pinnacle from far worse legal and reputational damage while creating community goodwill.

Our journey isn't about avoiding ethical crossroads altogether; it's about having a reliable compass when we find ourselves standing at one.

The stories of Daniel's response to the prayer decree and Valerie Brunswick's handling of environmental contamination reveal that addressing competing loyalties requires both clarity about our highest commitments and respect for legitimate organizational concerns. Their examples demonstrate how principled leadership, far from limiting organizational impact, often creates more sustainable solutions that serve genuine long-term interests.

But what happens when leaders face not only ethical dilemmas but also full-blown crises where resources are insufficient, time is short, and lives hang in the balance? In Chapter 7, we'll witness how Jeremiah provided ethical leadership during Jerusalem's siege and how Dr. Bridget Morrison applied similar principles during a modern medical crisis. Their stories demonstrate that moral clarity becomes even more essential, not less, in emergencies where expedient compromises seem most tempting.

SEVEN

CRISIS LEADERSHIP

The emergency operations center at Metropolitan Medical Center buzzed with a controlled urgency as Dr. Bridget Morrison surveyed the unfolding crisis. Twelve hours earlier, a catastrophic chemical plant explosion had sent toxic smoke billowing across the eastern part of the city. Hundreds of casualties had already arrived, overwhelming the hospital's capacity. More were expected as evacuation efforts continued in the affected neighborhoods.

Crisis preparation was more than a professional responsibility for Dr. Bridget Morrison; it was practically a personal philosophy. As Chief of Emergency Medicine, she combined the calm decisiveness of an experienced trauma surgeon with the organizational vision of a systems thinker. When chaos erupted, Bridget became the eye of the storm, a center of clarity to which others instinctively gravitated.

"Medicine is about preparing for what you hope never happens," she frequently told medical students. This perspective was shaped early in her career when she served with

Doctors Without Borders in conflict zones. There, she witnessed healthcare delivery under extreme resource constraints, experiences that instilled both pragmatic resourcefulness and an unwavering commitment to human dignity.

What distinguished Bridget from many other hospital administrators was her conviction that ethical principles became more essential during emergencies, not less. While some viewed moral considerations as luxuries that crisis situations couldn't afford, Bridget believed the opposite. "Our values matter most when resources are scarce and stakes are highest," she would insist in ethics committee meetings. This conviction would soon be tested in unprecedented ways when a catastrophic explosion at the chemical plant sent hundreds of casualties to the Metropolitan Medical Center, creating impossible demands on limited resources and forcing life-or-death decisions.

While previous chapters explored integrity, exposing corruption, surviving hostile environments, standing firm against authority, addressing ethical gray areas, and handling competing loyalties, this chapter examines a distinct challenge: maintaining ethical clarity during crisis situations. When resources are scarce and lives hang in the balance, how do we make decisions that preserve both effectiveness and moral principles? Jeremiah's leadership during Jerusalem's siege shows how ethical foundations become even more important during emergencies, not less.

As Chief of Emergency Medicine, Bridget had trained for mass casualty events throughout her career. However, no simulation could fully prepare anyone for the reality: the relentless flow of patients suffering from chemical burns and respiratory distress; frightened families searching for their loved ones; and exhausted staff pushing beyond normal limits, hour after hour.

"Dr. Morrison, we need your decision on resource allocation." Dr. Lawrence Blackwood, the hospital's CEO, approached with tense urgency. "We're running critically low on ventilators and specialized burn treatments. And the supply chain issues we've been facing mean replacements won't arrive for at least 48 hours."

Bridget examined the status boards displaying patient information throughout the emergency department and intensive care units. Every bed was occupied, and the overflow areas in the conference rooms and cafeteria were nearly at capacity. Ambulances continued to arrive at regular intervals.

"What about transfers to other facilities?" she asked.

"All regional hospitals are similarly overwhelmed," Lawrence replied. "And the road closures from the chemical release are complicating transport. We need to make decisions about the resources we have, not the ones we wish we had."

The unspoken question hung between them: How do you determine who receives potentially life-saving treatments when there aren't enough for everyone who needs them?

"I've assembled the hospital ethics committee," Lawrence continued. "They're waiting for your input on triage protocols." He hesitated. "The board is also concerned about our legal exposure if we implement crisis standards of care. They suggest we might need to prioritize patients with better legal standing."

Bridget understood the subtext immediately. The neighborhoods most affected by the chemical release were predominantly lower-income, with many undocumented residents.

Some board members suggested that limiting care for these patients could lower the hospital's legal and financial risks.

"The standard emergency triage protocols aren't designed for this duration or scale," Bridget acknowledged. "But any adjustments need to be based on medical criteria and potential for recovery, not demographics or legal status."

Lawrence frowned. "I understand the ethical position, Bridget. However, the hospital has financial and legal obligations that can't be ignored. Some board members are questioning whether we should even admit patients who can't provide identification or insurance information."

Bridget felt a surge of disbelief. "We're in the middle of a public health emergency. Turning away patients isn't just unethical —it's illegal under emergency care laws."

"The legal situation is more complex than that," Lawrence countered. "And the financial impact of this crisis could affect the hospital's ability to serve anyone in the future."

As Bridget contemplated her response, her pager sounded with another incoming trauma alert. "We need to continue this discussion," she said. "But right now, I have patients who need immediate attention."

As she hurried toward the emergency department entrance to meet the incoming ambulances, Bridget found her thoughts drifting to another time and place where crisis leadership required both practical wisdom and unwavering moral clarity...

JEREMIAH'S CRISIS LEADERSHIP

The dire situation in Jerusalem worsened day by day. Nebuchadnezzar's Babylonian army had besieged the city, cutting off food supplies and creating increasingly desperate conditions within the walls. The prophet Jeremiah, who had long warned of this judgment, now faced the practical realities of leadership during a prolonged crisis.

Though he was neither a king nor a military commander, Jeremiah exercised significant moral leadership during Jerusalem's darkest hour. His approach—particularly his willingness to speak unpopular truths while offering practical guidance for survival—provides a timeless model for ethical leadership in times of crisis.

As conditions in Jerusalem worsened, many leaders offered false hope, promising divine intervention without repentance and suggesting military alliances that would ultimately fail. The temptation to provide comforting falsehoods instead of difficult truths is powerful during crises when people desperately seek reassurance.

Jeremiah adopted a different approach. He unflinchingly acknowledged the reality of the situation: "This is what the Lord says: 'See, I am setting before you the way of life and the way of death. Whoever stays in this city will die by the sword, famine, or plague. But whoever goes out and surrenders to the Babylonians who are besieging you will live.'"

This message was so contrary to nationalistic sentiment that Jeremiah was accused of treason. Military officials complained to King Zedekiah: "This man should be put to death. He is discouraging the soldiers who are left in this city and all the people with the things he is saying to them. This man is not seeking the good of these people but their ruin."

With the king's permission, they cast Jeremiah into a cistern, where he sank into the mud and would have died without intervention from Ebed-Melek, an Ethiopian official who recognized the prophet's integrity and persuaded the king to authorize his rescue.

What is remarkable about Jeremiah's leadership during this crisis is his integration of moral clarity with practical guidance. He didn't merely pronounce judgment; he offered specific direction for those willing to listen: surrender to the Babylonians rather than prolong a hopeless resistance; purchase property as a sign of eventual restoration; and write to those already in exile with guidance for their survival and flourishing.

When a practical opportunity arose for his own safety, Jeremiah seized it. After Jerusalem fell, Nebuchadnezzar's commander, aware of Jeremiah's counsel to surrender, offered him protection and freedom. The prophet accepted this provision rather than adopting a stance of defiant suffering that would have served no purpose.

Throughout the prolonged crisis, Jeremiah maintained both moral clarity regarding the underlying causes of Jerusalem's situation and practical wisdom on how to respond to immediate realities. He did not allow immediate pressures to compromise his message, nor did he retreat into abstract principles without addressing practical needs.

Perhaps most notably, Jeremiah balanced unflinching truthtelling with deep compassion. The same prophet who delivered messages of judgment wrote: "My eyes fail with tears, my heart is troubled; my bile is poured on the ground because of the destruction of the daughter of my people, because the children and the infants faint in the streets of the city."

This integration of moral clarity, practical wisdom, and genuine compassion made Jeremiah's leadership during crises highly effective, even when his counsel was initially rejected. When Jerusalem ultimately fell, as he had predicted, many survivors recognized the integrity of his guidance and sought him out for direction in the aftermath.

STANDING FIRM IN A MEDICAL CRISIS

As Dr. Bridget Morrison directed the care of newly arrived patients with chemical burns and respiratory distress, she drew insight from Jeremiah's example. Like him, she faced a crisis where truth might be unwelcome but was nevertheless essential. She needed to balance moral clarity with practical realities, and she required the courage to uphold her values even when doing so created personal risk.

Three hours later, after stabilizing the latest arrivals, Bridget joined the hospital ethics committee meeting that was already underway. The tension in the room was palpable as physicians, nurses, administrators, and ethicists grappled with the unavoidable allocation decisions.

"We need a medically sound and ethically defensible system," the committee chair said as Bridget took her seat. "The question is how to prioritize when we can't provide optimal care to everyone."

"The scoring system proposed by the administration gives weight to long-term recovery potential and social factors," another committee member noted, gesturing toward a document being distributed. "Including insurance status and legal residence."

Bridget reviewed the proposed protocol with growing concern. While it included valid medical criteria, it also included factors that would systematically disadvantage the most vulnerable patients—those from the communities most affected by the chemical release.

When it was her turn to speak, Bridget chose her words carefully. Like Jeremiah addressing Jerusalem's leaders, she needed to express the reality clearly without compromising essential principles.

"I understand the unprecedented pressures we're facing," she began. "And I recognize that crisis standards of care require difficult choices. But our guiding principle must remain the same in crisis as in normal times: we provide care based on medical need, not social status."

She turned to Lawrence Blackwood. "I've reviewed our supply situation and current patient load. We're stretched beyond capacity, but there are options we haven't fully explored."

Bridget outlined a three-part approach: reorganizing specialized teams to maximize efficiency, implementing a resource-sharing arrangement with the veterans' hospital across the city, which had been less affected by the crisis, and utilizing alternative treatments when standard methods weren't available.

"These steps won't eliminate the need for difficult decisions," she acknowledged. "But they will expand our capacity while maintaining our core ethical commitments."

"That's all well and good," one administrator objected, "but it doesn't address the financial reality. This crisis could bankrupt the hospital if we don't consider the economics of each admission."

"First, providing care without discrimination during a declared emergency is our legal obligation, not just our ethical one," Bridget countered. "Second, disaster funding will help address the financial impact, but only if we can demonstrate we followed appropriate protocols. Creating a policy that explicitly discriminates based on social factors would jeopardize that funding and expose us to lawsuits that would far exceed the cost of care."

She paused, then continued with the moral heart of her argument: "Most importantly, if we abandon our fundamental commitment to treating each patient based on medical need, we've lost something more valuable than money. We've lost our identity as healthcare providers and our trust with the community we serve."

The debate continued for another hour, with various committee members expressing concerns about resource limitations, staff burnout, and long-term financial viability. Throughout the discussion, Bridget acknowledged these legitimate issues while upholding her core position: the hospital would not adopt triage criteria that systematically disadvantaged vulnerable populations.

Like Jeremiah, who recognized the practical realities of Jerusalem's situation while refusing to compromise his essential message, Bridget balanced pragmatism with principle. She acknowledged that perfect care for all was impossible in the current crisis but rejected the notion that expedient discrimination was therefore necessary or justified.

When the meeting concluded, the committee adopted a modified protocol that incorporated Bridget's resource-expansion strategies while maintaining medically appropriate triage criteria without social discrimination. However, the victory felt fragile. Several administrators remained clearly skeptical, and Lawrence's expression suggested that the board might still intervene.

As she left the meeting to return to the emergency department, Bridget was stopped by Sebastian Barrett, the CEO of a major manufacturing company and chairman of the hospital's board of directors. His presence at the hospital during the crisis was unusual, indicating a significant concern about the situation.

"Dr. Morrison, do you have a moment?" he asked, gesturing toward an empty conference room.

Once inside, with the door closed, Barrett's demeanor was grave. "I understand you've taken a strong position against considering financial factors in our triage decisions."

"I've advocated for medically appropriate criteria without social discrimination," Bridget clarified.

"A noble sentiment," Barrett replied. "But perhaps impractical given the magnitude of this crisis. The board has serious concerns about the hospital's financial exposure, particularly regarding undocumented patients who may lack legal standing to sue if care is delayed or limited."

The implication was clear: the board was considering overriding the ethics committee's decision.

Bridget felt the full weight of the moment. Her response could determine care for hundreds of patients in the current crisis and set precedents for future emergencies. Drawing from Jeremiah's example, she chose to speak the truth directly yet respectfully:

"Mr. Barrett, I understand the board's fiduciary responsibility. But what you're suggesting isn't just ethically problematic—it's legally indefensible and practically short-sighted."

She outlined the emergency care laws that prohibited discrimination, the disaster funding requirements that would be jeopardized by documented discrimination, and the community trust that would be irreparably damaged if the hospital abandoned its core mission during a public health emergency.

"Beyond the legal and practical issues," she concluded, "there's a fundamental question of who we are as an institution. Metropolitan was founded to serve this entire community, especially in times of greatest need. If we abandon that commitment when it's tested, what remains of our purpose?"

Barrett studied her thoughtfully. "You feel strongly about this."

"I do," Bridget acknowledged. "And I would be forced to document my objections if the board overrides the ethics committee decision. Not as a threat, but as a matter of professional responsibility."

The implicit message was clear: if the board insisted on discriminatory practices, a paper trail would emerge, potentially leading to significant legal and reputational consequences. Like Jeremiah before King Zedekiah, Bridget spoke the truth regardless of personal risk.

After a long moment, Barrett nodded slowly. "I'll convey your perspective to the board. In the meantime, continue with the protocols approved by the ethics committee."

It wasn't an unequivocal victory, but it offered an opportunity to implement a more ethical approach while the board deliberated.

As Bridget returned to the emergency department, she felt both the weight of the ongoing crisis and a sense of clarity regarding her path forward.

The next seventy-two hours tested everyone at Metropolitan Medical Center. The patient flow continued unabated. The staff worked well beyond their normal limits. Resources remained critically constrained despite creative reallocation efforts. Difficult triage decisions had to be made hourly.

Throughout this period, Bridget maintained a leadership presence that balanced her unwavering ethical commitment with practical adaptability. Like Jeremiah during Jerusalem's siege, she didn't pretend the situation was better than it was; however, she also did not abandon hope or principle in the face of overwhelming challenges.

When ventilators became scarce, she implemented a protocol for carefully timed sharing between patients whose conditions permitted it. When burn treatment supplies dwindled, she collaborated with pharmacists to adapt alternative formulations. When staff reached the point of exhaustion, she reorganized schedules to ensure rest periods while maintaining essential coverage.

Perhaps most importantly, Bridget maintained open communication throughout the crisis. In daily briefings, she candidly acknowledged the challenges while highlighting the extraordinary efforts being made. She frequently visited every treatment area, listening to concerns and explaining decisions clearly and compassionately.

Four days into the crisis, the situation began to stabilize. The chemical release had been contained, and the evacuation of affected areas was complete. Patient flow slowed from a flood to a steady stream. Regional supply chains started to recover, bringing in needed resources.

In the aftermath, as the hospital returned to normal operations, Bridget was surprised to receive a request to meet with Sebastian Barrett and the executive committee of the board. Anticipating criticism of her stance during the crisis, she prepared her defense regarding the decisions made under her leadership.

When she entered the boardroom, however, the atmosphere wasn't confrontational. Barrett greeted her with unexpected warmth.

"Dr. Morrison, we've asked you here to express our appreciation," he began. "Your leadership during this crisis exemplified the highest standards of medical ethics and practical effectiveness. The protocols you implemented saved lives while preserving the hospital's core values."

Bridget was momentarily speechless.

Barrett continued, "I'll be honest—many of us, myself included, questioned whether maintaining non-discriminatory practices was realistic given the resource constraints. We were wrong. Your approach not only protected vulnerable patients but also positioned the hospital for stronger community support and clearer disaster funding claims than alternative approaches would have allowed."

An in-depth discussion ensued regarding lessons learned from the crisis and the investments required to enhance future emergency response capabilities. The board, having witnessed the effectiveness of ethically sound practices even under extreme pressure, was now committed to supporting infrastructure that would ensure those practices are more sustainable.

In the months that followed, Metropolitan Medical Center implemented numerous improvements based on insights gained from the chemical release crisis. New emergency protocols were developed with clear ethical frameworks. Staff received enhanced training in crisis resource management. Community partnerships were strengthened to provide better coordination during future emergencies.

Bridget found herself in an expanded leadership role, asked to share the hospital's experiences at national conferences and contribute to developing regional disaster response plans. Like Jeremiah, whose guidance became even more valued after Jerusalem's fall confirmed his wisdom, her commitment to both practical effectiveness and ethical integrity during crises enhanced rather than diminished her influence.

THE CRISIS LEADERSHIP CYCLE: LESSONS FROM JEREMIAH AND DR. MORRISON

Building on the foundation of integrity (Chapter 1), the courage to expose wrongdoing (Chapter 2), resilience in hostile environments (Chapter 3), firmness when facing authority (Chapter 4), wisdom in ethical gray areas (Chapter 5), and clarity in competing loyalties (Chapter 6), we now add the final element to our ethical leadership blueprint: maintaining moral clarity during crisis situations.

The stories of Jeremiah during Jerusalem's siege and Dr. Bridget Morrison during the chemical release crisis reveal powerful insights about leading with integrity in emergencies. Although separated by millennia, their parallel journeys illuminate how ethical clarity becomes even more essential when resources are limited and lives hang in the balance.

Crisis leadership begins long before an emergency strikes. Both Jeremiah and Dr. Morrison established clear ethical foundations that served as decision-making anchors when pressure intensified. Jeremiah's lifelong commitment to truth-telling provided him with clarity during Jerusalem's darkest hours. Similarly, Dr. Morrison's deep-rooted commitment to equitable patient care offered an unwavering compass when expedient alternatives arose.

Notice also how relationship building played a key role. Jeremiah cultivated connections with key figures like Ebed-Melek, who later intervened to save his life. Dr. Morrison likewise built coalitions with medical staff and board members who became essential allies during the critical decision-making process. These networks didn't emerge spontaneously during the crisis but were cultivated through consistent ethical practice beforehand.

When crises struck, both leaders demonstrated several key attributes that allowed them to maintain ethical clarity amid chaos. They offered unflinching assessments of reality, refusing to provide false reassurances. They engaged in creative problem-solving rather than accepting binary choices. Jeremiah provided practical guidance for surviving exile while maintaining cultural identity. Dr. Morrison developed resource-sharing arrangements with other facilities while upholding non-discriminatory care principles.

Perhaps most importantly, both maintained transparent communication, speaking difficult truths directly to those in power. This created trust even when delivering unwelcome messages. They balanced honesty about limitations with a hopeful framing that inspired rather than demoralized their communities.

The aftermath of each crisis revealed that ethical leadership creates unexpected positive outcomes that compromise never achieves. Jeremiah's uncompromising stance earned him protection and the opportunity to guide survivors. Dr. Morrison's principled approach strengthened her leadership position and expanded her role in shaping future crisis protocols. Neither leader just weathered their crisis; they improved systems for the future, establishing legacies of integrity that outlasted the immediate emergency.

PREPARING YOUR LEADERSHIP FOR CRISIS

Crisis situations, unlike other ethical challenges that develop gradually, require an immediate response based on limited information. Consider these practical approaches to enhance your crisis leadership capabilities:

Create a personal crisis compass by identifying your non-negotiable values that will guide crisis decisions. Write them down now, before pressure distorts your thinking. These are not abstract ideals but concrete principles that will direct resource allocation when needs exceed capacity.

Develop your stakeholder network before you need it. Who are the key allies you would require during an ethical crisis in your organization? Have you invested in those relationships before needing their support? A crisis is the wrong time to start building trust.

Prepare your communication strategy. How prepared are you to speak truth to power when resources are limited? Can you remain transparent without inciting panic? Will you inspire hope while recognizing difficult realities? These skills need practice before a crisis occurs.

Consider creating practical tools, such as a decision journal where you record significant ethical choices and their outcomes. This method fosters pattern recognition, which accelerates decision-making during emergency situations. Some leaders even devise a pocket-sized reminder of core ethical principles that they can reference during high-pressure moments.

Finally, identify your crisis cabinet: 3 to 5 trusted advisors with complementary perspectives whom you can call upon during ethical emergencies. These individuals should offer diverse viewpoints while sharing your commitment to core values.

The wisdom that Jeremiah and Dr. Morrison demonstrate isn't theoretical but practical. They show us that ethical leadership in crisis isn't about having perfect answers but about maintaining core values while adapting to emergency conditions. Their examples remind us that how we lead during our most challenging moments often defines our legacy far more than our actions during times of stability and plenty.

A crisis doesn't define our ethical character; it reveals it. The preparations you make today will shape your ability to lead with both integrity and effectiveness when confronting your own unavoidable moments of truth.

Ethical clarity during crisis creates outcomes that expedient compromise never could.

Jeremiah's unflinching truth-telling during Jerusalem's crisis and Dr. Bridget Morrison's principled leadership during the chemical release emergency illustrate that ethical leadership in crises requires both moral clarity and practical wisdom. Their examples demonstrate how maintaining core values while adapting to emergency conditions creates more sustainable outcomes than expedient compromise ever could.

But how do ancient ethical frameworks like Daniel's apply to the cutting-edge challenges of our digital age? In Chapter 8, we'll explore how Daniel's blueprint for ethical leadership illuminates contemporary issues in technology, artificial intelligence, and digital transformation. We'll meet Dr. Evelyn Lancaster, whose application of Daniel's principles to modern tech ethics demonstrates that while our tools have changed dramatically, fundamental questions about truth, power, responsibility, and human dignity remain remarkably consistent.

EIGHT
THE MODERN RELEVANCE OF DANIEL'S ETHICAL LEGACY

The Stanford Ethics in Technology Institute lecture hall fell silent as Dr. Evelyn Lancaster approached the podium. As one of the world's leading experts on ethical artificial intelligence, her annual lecture attracted a full audience of students, faculty, industry leaders, and policymakers. This year's topic had raised eyebrows when announced: "Ancient Wisdom for Modern Technology: Daniel's Blueprint for Ethical Leadership in the Digital Age."

The dividing lines between disciplines that seemed so clear to others had always appeared artificial to Dr. Evelyn Lancaster. With advanced degrees in both computer science and philosophy, she moved between technological innovation and ethical reflection with unusual fluidity. This intellectual versatility made her one of the world's leading experts on ethical artificial intelligence.

"Technology shapes our humanity, and our humanity should shape our technology," she often said during her popular university lectures. This integrated perspective had roots in her childhood, growing up with a theologian mother and a physicist father who engaged in fascinating dinner table conversations about meaning, purpose, and scientific discovery.

What made Evelyn's approach particularly valuable was not just her interdisciplinary background but also her ability to connect ancient wisdom with cutting-edge challenges. While many tech ethicists relied primarily on abstract frameworks, Evelyn drew meaningful connections between timeless human questions and emerging technological capabilities. This unique approach has earned her both respect and occasional skepticism from purely technical colleagues. It will soon be put to the test when she is invited to address quantum computing pioneers about ethical approaches for technologies with unprecedented power.

While previous chapters applied Daniel's blueprint to traditional ethical challenges—maintaining integrity, exposing corruption, surviving hostile environments, standing firm against authority, addressing ethical gray areas, managing competing loyalties, and preserving clarity during crises—this chapter explores how these ancient principles apply to cutting-edge technology. Can wisdom from millennia ago guide us in governing artificial intelligence, quantum computing, and digital platforms? Evelyn Lancaster's work demonstrates how timeless ethical principles remain relevant even as our technological capabilities advance exponentially.

"Some of you may be wondering," she began with a knowing smile, "why a scientist and ethicist with degrees from MIT and Oxford is invoking a biblical figure to address cutting-edge technological challenges. It's a fair question."

She removed her glasses, making direct eye contact with the audience.

"I've spent twenty years working at the intersection of technology and ethics. I've advised governments, corporations, and international bodies on how we might harness the powerful capabilities of artificial intelligence while protecting human flourishing. And I've come to a somewhat unexpected conclusion."

She paused, allowing the anticipation to build.

"The fundamental ethical challenges we face aren't new. The exponential growth of our technological capabilities has merely amplified age-old questions regarding power, truth, integrity, and human dignity. Sometimes, ancient wisdom provides surprisingly relevant guidance for addressing these heightened dilemmas."

During her Stanford Ethics in Technology lectures, Evelyn often drew parallels between contemporary tech challenges and historical ethical frameworks. The ancient story of Daniel had proven particularly resonant with her students, many of whom would go on to careers at companies like Quantum Dynamics.

"Consider Daniel as history's first documented ethical advisor to power," she would suggest. "He maintained integrity while making his expertise genuinely useful."

Now, facing skepticism from Katherine Whitman about applying 'biblical ethics' to quantum computing, Evelyn needed to demonstrate how ancient wisdom could illuminate cutting-edge technological dilemmas without imposing particular religious viewpoints.

Evelyn tapped her tablet's screen, revealing an image of an ancient Babylonian relief sculpture depicting court officials before a king.

"Consider Daniel, a young exile in the court of Babylon during the 6th century BCE. Transported from his homeland to serve in a foreign empire, he addressed a complex ethical terrain where power was concentrated, the consequences for principled stands were severe, and the pressure to compromise was constant."

She moved to the next slide, showcasing a modern data center with rows of gleaming servers.

"Today, we face a new kind of empire—the unprecedented concentration of information, wealth, and influence within our technological infrastructure. Like ancient Babylon, this digital empire offers remarkable benefits. Also like Babylon, it presents significant ethical challenges for those who work within it."

Evelyn's gaze swept across the audience, noting the mix of skepticism and interest. In the front row, she recognized Katherine Whitman, the CEO of Quantum Dynamics, whose groundbreaking work in quantum computing had turned her into a reluctant celebrity in the tech world. Katherine's expression was guarded but attentive.

"Daniel's experiences in Babylon offer a model for ethical leadership that translates with surprising relevance to our digital age," Evelyn continued. "Let's examine four specific incidents from his story and their modern parallels."

She moved to a slide showing a split image: on one side, an ancient banquet hall, and on the other, a modern corporate boardroom.

"First, consider the famous story of the writing on the wall. King Belshazzar hosts an extravagant banquet, using sacred vessels looted from Jerusalem's temple—a display of power that shows no respect for boundaries. Supernatural writing appears on the wall, and only Daniel can interpret it. His message to the king is direct: 'You have been weighed on the scales and found wanting.' That very night, Babylon falls to the Persians."

Evelyn looked up from her notes.

"The parallel to our time is striking. We've built digital platforms of unprecedented scale and power. We've disrupted industries, changed social interactions, and reshaped economies—often with inadequate concern for ethical boundaries. And now, increasingly, the writing is appearing on our wall."

She clicked on a slide that displayed headlines about controversies in technology ethics, including privacy violations, algorithmic bias, the mental health impacts of social media, and election manipulation.

"The second Daniel story worth examining is his refusal to eat the king's food. This might seem trivial compared to later life-threatening stands, but it established a pattern. Daniel recognized that seemingly small compromises often pave the way for larger ones. By drawing a clear line on a 'minor' issue, he developed the ethical muscle and credibility that would serve him in greater challenges."

Evelyn noticed Katherine Whitman shifting uncomfortably in her seat. The quantum computing pioneer had recently faced criticism for accepting defense contracts that some ethicists argued crossed significant boundaries.

"In our technological context," Evelyn continued, "we face many seemingly 'small' ethical choices: collecting a bit more user data than necessary, designing for engagement rather than well-being, and allowing minor biases in algorithms to persist because fixing them would delay deployment. Daniel reminds us that these small choices establish patterns that shape our response to larger ethical challenges."

She moved to a slide depicting Daniel before King Darius, with modern executives in a regulatory hearing on the opposite side.

"The third instructive incident is Daniel's response to the prayer decree—a law specifically designed to trap him in a conflict between political loyalty and spiritual integrity. Rather than capitulating or mounting a rebellion, Daniel maintains his spiritual practice exactly as before, accepting the consequences of his principled stand. His unwavering integrity ultimately brings about systemic change when Darius issues a new decree protecting religious freedom."

Evelyn looked directly at the industry leaders in her audience.

"How many of us in the technology sector have found ourselves in situations where organizational expectations conflict with our deeper values? Daniel's example challenges us to maintain integrity even when doing so carries professional risk, and reminds us that principled stands often create ripple effects beyond what we can initially see."

Katherine Whitman was now taking notes, her expression thoughtful. Evelyn had heard rumors that Quantum Dynamics was struggling with ethical guidelines for their revolutionary technology, which could potentially compromise all existing encryption systems.

"Finally," Evelyn continued, "consider Daniel's interpretations of Nebuchadnezzar's dreams. When the king demands that his advisors tell him both the content of his forgotten dream and its interpretation—an impossible task—Daniel acknowledges his limitations while pointing to a higher source of wisdom. He doesn't claim special powers but serves as a conduit for insight beyond himself."

She paused, letting the point settle.

"In an age of unprecedented technological capability, this humility is perhaps Daniel's most countercultural example. Our digital tools create an illusion of omniscience and omnipotence that can blind us to our limitations. Daniel reminds us that wisdom often requires acknowledging what we don't know and cannot control."

Evelyn set aside her notes and addressed the audience more directly.

"These ancient stories might seem remote from neural networks and quantum computing. But the ethical principles they illustrate—speaking truth to power, maintaining integrity under pressure, accepting consequences for principled stands, and practicing humility amid capability—are exactly what our technological age most desperately needs."

As she opened the floor for questions, hands shot up throughout the lecture hall. For the next forty-five minutes, Evelyn engaged in a lively dialogue with students, faculty, and industry representatives about the practical application of these principles to specific technological challenges.

The final question came from Katherine Whitman herself.

"Dr. Lancaster, you've made a compelling case for the relevance of Daniel's ethical approach," the quantum computing pioneer acknowledged. "But Daniel had clear religious principles guiding his decisions. How do we find common ethical ground without imposing particular religious viewpoints in our pluralistic industry with diverse beliefs?"

It was the question Evelyn had been waiting for—the one that always arose when she connected ancient wisdom with modern ethics. Her response would determine whether the concepts she had presented would be embraced or dismissed by the very leaders who needed to hear them the most.

"That's precisely why Daniel's example is so valuable, Dr. Whitman," she replied. "He maintained his principles without imposing them on others. He didn't demand that the Babylonians adopt Jewish practices or beliefs. He simply lived his values consistently while contributing his best work to the society where he was placed."

Evelyn stepped from behind the podium, closing the distance between herself and the audience.

"The principles I've highlighted today—truth-telling, integrity, principled stands, and humility—can be derived from many ethical traditions, both religious and secular. Daniel's particular motivation was his faith, but the wisdom of his approach transcends any single belief system."

She looked around the room, making eye contact with as many attendees as possible.

"The question isn't whether we should impose biblical ethics on technology companies. The question is whether we can extract timeless wisdom from many sources, including ancient ones, to address modern challenges. Daniel's story continues to resonate not because everyone shares his religious beliefs, but because his embodied ethical principles speak to fundamental human values across cultures and centuries."

The response was a thoughtful silence, followed by heartfelt applause. As Evelyn collected her materials, Katherine Whitman approached the podium.

"I'd like to continue this conversation," the quantum computing CEO said. "My team is wrestling with ethical guidelines for technology that could potentially break all existing encryption. The approach you've outlined might help us address these waters."

Evelyn replied, "I'd be happy to meet," recognizing the significance of this opening. Katherine Whitman was notoriously resistant to external ethical guidance, preferring to set her own course. This willingness to engage represented a remarkable opportunity.

APPLYING ANCIENT WISDOM TO QUANTUM COMPUTING

Two days later, Evelyn found herself in the minimalist headquarters of Quantum Dynamics, seated across from Katherine in a glass-walled conference room overlooking the San Francisco Bay. Several senior executives and research leaders from the company joined them, their expressions reflecting a mix of curiosity and skepticism.

Katherine began, "I appreciated your lecture, but I'm still not convinced that ancient wisdom applies to quantum computing. We're dealing with technological capabilities that would have been incomprehensible in Daniel's time."

"The technologies are certainly new," Evelyn acknowledged, "but the ethical questions aren't. Who should have access to power? What responsibilities come with specialized knowledge? How do we balance advancement with potential harm?

Daniel wrestled with these same questions in the context of his era."

Katherine nodded toward a digital display showing complex quantum algorithms.

"Our latest breakthrough could potentially render all current encryption obsolete. Every secured system on the planet— banking, government communications, personal data—could be vulnerable. The security implications are staggering."

"Which makes the ethical questions all the more critical," Evelyn noted. "How will you manage this capability? Who decides when and how it's deployed? What safeguards will prevent misuse?"

"We've been debating these questions for months," one of the research leaders admitted. "There are compelling arguments on all sides. National security agencies want priority access. Commercial applications could be enormously profitable. But the potential for misuse is equally enormous."

Evelyn contemplated how Daniel's example might shed light on this very modern dilemma.

"When Daniel received insight into Nebuchadnezzar's dream —information that carried significant power—he did several noteworthy things. First, he acknowledged that the wisdom came through him but not from him, maintaining humility despite his capability. Second, he used his insight to serve both the king and the broader community, not for personal advantage. Third, he spoke truth about the dream's implications, even when that truth was unwelcome."

She looked directly at Katherine.

"These principles translate remarkably well to your current situation. Acknowledge that with great capability comes great responsibility. Use your breakthrough to serve broad human flourishing, not merely organizational interests. And be unflinchingly honest about both the benefits and risks of this technology, even when that honesty might be commercially inconvenient."

The ensuing conversation was intense and wide-ranging. The Quantum Dynamics team raised practical concerns regarding market pressures, competitive dynamics, and fiduciary responsibilities to shareholders. Evelyn acknowledged these realities while consistently redirecting the discussion towards fundamental ethical principles.

She reminded them, "Daniel didn't live in a theoretical world either. He operated within the constraints of a very real empire with very real power dynamics. His ability to find creative paths that honored both practical realities and deeper principles distinguished him."

By the end of the meeting, no final decisions had been made, but a model was emerging. Katherine proposed a multi-stakeholder ethics council to oversee the deployment of the encryption-breaking technology, which would include representatives from security experts, privacy advocates, government, and the broader tech community. Access would be carefully controlled, featuring transparent oversight mechanisms and regular ethical audits.

Katherine acknowledged as she walked Evelyn to the elevator, "It's not perfect, but it's a start. Without this approach, I suspect we would have defaulted to what most benefits us competitively."

"That's how ethical progress typically happens," Evelyn replied. "Not through perfect solutions but through better approaches than would otherwise have emerged. Daniel didn't create a perfect system in Babylon, but he influenced it toward greater wisdom and justice than it would have had without him."

As she rode the elevator down to the lobby, Evelyn reflected on how this engagement exemplified her broader mission: helping contemporary leaders recognize the relevance of ancient wisdom to modern challenges. The specifics of quantum computing would have been incomprehensible to Daniel, but the ethical principles he embodied continued to guide her in addressing the use of powerful capabilities.

EXPANDING ETHICAL INFLUENCE

Half a year later, Evelyn received an email from Katherine Whitman that included a link to a press release. Quantum Dynamics had announced both its breakthrough and the ethical approach for managing it. The multi-stakeholder council was established with clear governance principles that balanced advancement and responsibility. Security researchers, privacy advocates, and policy experts cautiously praised the approach as a model for managing potentially disruptive technologies.

"Your DANIEL approach proved more applicable than I initially thought," Katherine wrote. "Particularly the principle of acknowledging that wisdom flows through us but not from us. It helped us recognize that just because we can develop certain capabilities doesn't mean we should decide how they're deployed alone."

The email continued: "We've been invited to present our governance model at next month's International Cybersecurity Conference. I'd appreciate it if you would join our panel to discuss the ethical principles that shaped our approach."

This invitation represented a significant opportunity to influence the governance of emerging technologies. Evelyn had spent years trying to integrate ethical principles into technological development earlier in the process, rather than as an afterthought. The Quantum Dynamics case could exemplify this approach in action.

As she prepared for the conference, Evelyn reflected on the parallels between Daniel's influence in ancient Babylon and her own work in the modern technological landscape. Daniel had not set out to reform the entire Babylonian empire; he had simply maintained his integrity while offering his best insights where he was placed. Yet, his influence eventually extended far beyond what he could have initially imagined, affecting imperial decrees and policies that shaped the lives of countless people.

Similarly, Evelyn hadn't anticipated that her Stanford lecture would catalyze a new ethical approach for groundbreaking technology. She had simply shared her best insights, drawing from both ancient and modern sources, to illuminate contemporary challenges. Yet that offering sparked changes that could potentially shape how powerful capabilities are governed globally.

At the cybersecurity conference, the panel discussion drew an overflow crowd of security professionals, technology leaders, and policy experts. Katherine began with a clear explanation of their quantum computing breakthrough and its implications for existing encryption systems. She then outlined the ethical approach they had developed, explicitly acknowledging its roots in the ancient wisdom Evelyn had shared.

"We recognize that with unprecedented capability comes unprecedented responsibility," Katherine explained. "By implementing a governance model that includes diverse perspectives and transparent oversight, we are trying to ensure that this technology serves human flourishing rather than undermining it."

When it was Evelyn's turn to speak, she focused on the broader implications of this approach.

"What Quantum Dynamics has demonstrated is that ethical principles don't hinder technological advancement—they guide it toward more beneficial outcomes. By integrating ethical considerations early in the development process, rather than as an afterthought, they've created a model that advances both technological capability and human welfare."

The questions from the audience revealed both interest in the approach and skepticism about its broader applicability. Some suggested it would work only for established companies with the resources to support elaborate governance structures. Others questioned whether it would survive contact with market realities and competitive pressures.

Evelyn acknowledged these concerns while emphasizing the core principles that could be adapted to various contexts.

"The specifics of implementation will vary by organization, industry, and technology. But the fundamental ethical principles—truthful acknowledgment of impacts, integrity in development and deployment, accepting responsibility for consequences, and humility about our own limitations—apply regardless of scale or specific capabilities."

In the months and years that followed, the "DANIEL Approach," as it came to be known in technology ethics circles, gained traction among companies and organizations developing powerful new capabilities. Although it didn't solve all ethical challenges, it offered a structured method for addressing them earlier and more systematically than was previously common.

Evelyn continued her work at the Ethics in Technology Institute, advising organizations and speaking at conferences around the globe. She maintained regular contact with Katherine Whitman, whose experience in implementing the approach at Quantum Dynamics offered valuable insights for refining and expanding the method.

Five years after her Stanford lecture, Evelyn published a book titled "Ancient Wisdom for Digital Empires: Ethical Leadership in the Age of Powerful Technology." The book expanded on the DANIEL Approach and incorporated case studies from various organizations that had implemented it. Katherine Whitman contributed the foreword, describing how ancient principles guided their approach to modern technological capabilities.

The book's final chapter reflects on why ancient wisdom remains relevant in rapidly changing technological environments.

"The specific capabilities change dramatically over time," Evelyn wrote, "but the fundamental questions about how we use power, pursue truth, maintain integrity, and respect human dignity remain remarkably constant. Daniel's example reminds us that ethical leadership is not about having perfect answers to these questions, but about approaching them with both principled commitment and practical wisdom."

She continued: "In an age of accelerating technological change, we need this dual commitment more than ever. We need the moral clarity to recognize which values must be maintained regardless of technological capability, and the practical wisdom to apply those values in rapidly evolving contexts. Daniel demonstrated this integration of principle and pragmatism in ancient Babylon. Our challenge is to demonstrate it in our modern digital empires."

The book concluded with a call to action for those working in technology:

"You may not think of yourselves as modern Daniels, interpreting dreams and facing lions. But like him, you work within systems of enormous power and influence. Like him, you face pressures to compromise principles for expediency. Like him, you have opportunities to shape how power is used in ways that affect countless lives. And like him, your greatest contribution may not be the specific capabilities you develop, but the wisdom and integrity you bring to their governance and deployment."

TIMELESS PRINCIPLES FOR MODERN TECHNOLOGY

Building on the earlier elements of Daniel's ethical blueprint—integrity under pressure (Chapter 1), exposing corruption (Chapter 2), resilience in hostile environments (Chapter 3), standing firm against authority (Chapter 4), wisdom in ethical gray areas (Chapter 5), clarity in competing loyalties (Chapter 6), and moral clarity during crises (Chapter 7)—we now see how these principles apply across technological eras. The ethical wisdom Daniel demonstrated in ancient Babylon proves remarkably applicable to our digital age.

The stories of Daniel in ancient Babylon and Dr. Evelyn Lancaster in the modern technological landscape reveal enduring principles about ethical leadership across vastly different eras. Though separated by millennia and radically different contexts, their experiences demonstrate how ancient wisdom can illuminate contemporary challenges.

First, both stories illustrate that fundamental ethical questions transcend technological and cultural changes. Daniel grappled with the appropriate use of power, the importance of truth-telling, the maintenance of integrity under pressure, and the proper boundaries of human authority. These same questions recur today, albeit with new technological complexities. Recognizing these continuities helps us understand that we are not facing entirely unprecedented ethical terrain, even amid extraordinary technological capabilities.

Second, we see that ethical principles need not impose specific religious or cultural viewpoints to draw wisdom from ancient sources. Daniel upheld his particular faith commitments without demanding that others adopt them. Evelyn presented principles derived from Daniel's example in language accessible to diverse audiences without requiring adherence to his specific religious beliefs. Ancient wisdom can be translated into terms relevant to pluralistic modern contexts without losing its essential insights.

Third, both examples illustrate the catalytic impact of individuals who maintain ethical clarity within powerful systems. Daniel's consistent integrity influenced the policies and practices of numerous empires. Inspired by Daniel's example, Evelyn's approach shaped how organizations governed powerful technologies. Neither aimed primarily to reform systems; yet both significantly influenced them through principled engagement from within.

Fourth, we observe the integration of moral commitment with practical wisdom. Daniel didn't merely pronounce ethical absolutes; he discovered innovative ways to apply principles within the constraints of real-world systems. Evelyn didn't present abstract ethical theories disconnected from technological realities; she created practical methods that organizations could genuinely implement. This fusion of principle and pragmatism made their ethical leadership effective rather than merely idealistic.

As you address challenges in your professional setting, particularly in fields changed by powerful new capabilities, the enduring relevance of ancient wisdom offers valuable guidance. The specific technologies you work with may bear little resemblance to anything Daniel would have recognized, but the ethical questions underlying their development and use would be surprisingly familiar to him.

Consider asking yourself:

- What fundamental human values must be preserved regardless of technological capability? Just as Daniel maintained his core commitments despite pressure to compromise, which principles should remain non-negotiable amid technological change?
- How can I translate these values into approaches that resonate in diverse, pluralistic contexts? Like Evelyn presenting Daniel's example to a modern audience, how can you convey ethical insights in a language accessible to those who do not share your specific worldview?
- Where can I find opportunities to influence systems from within through principled engagement? Daniel shaped Babylonian and Persian policies not through

revolution but through consistent integrity in his designated role. Where could your unwavering ethical leadership create similar ripple effects?

- How can I integrate moral commitment with practical wisdom in my specific context? Daniel and Evelyn found ways to apply principles that acknowledged real-world constraints without compromising core values. What might this integration look like in your professional setting?

The accelerating pace of technological change can create the illusion that we are in entirely uncharted ethical territory. This perception often leads either to ethical paralysis (because the challenges seem overwhelming) or to ethical relativism (because traditional frameworks seem outdated). Daniel's example, reinterpreted for our time, offers an alternative: ethical wisdom that acknowledges both the continuity of fundamental human values and the need for creative application in new contexts.

Most importantly, remember that your ethical influence may extend far beyond what you can currently envision. Daniel couldn't have anticipated how his faithful service in Babylon would inspire ethical reflection millennia later. Evelyn couldn't have predicted how her Stanford lecture would shape the governance of quantum computing. Your consistent commitment to ethical leadership within your sphere of influence can create ripples that reach further and last longer than you imagine.

Consider this: what matters most isn't if you'll encounter situations that challenge your principles, but how prepared you'll be to uphold them when you do.

Timeless ethical principles create responsible innovation that technological capability alone never could.

Dr. Evelyn Lancaster's application of Daniel's ethical principles to quantum computing challenges demonstrates that ancient wisdom retains significant relevance for our most modern technologies. Although the specific contexts differ dramatically, the fundamental questions about ethical boundaries, speaking truth to power, and responsible stewardship of influence transcend time and technological change.

But maintaining ethical leadership isn't just about addressing individual challenges; it's about developing the capacity for moral consistency throughout an entire career. How did Daniel uphold his integrity not only in isolated incidents but also through decades of service amidst multiple regimes and escalating challenges?

In Chapter 9, we'll explore the concept of ethical resilience through the contrasting stories of Daniel's lifelong integrity and Philip Holbrook's journey of moral rebuilding after ethical collapse.

NINE

ETHICAL RESILIENCE

The prison visiting room buzzed with muted conversations as Caroline Prescott straightened her blazer and waited for her former mentee to arrive. After forty years of leading organizations through ethical change, she now devotes her time to mentoring leaders facing complex moral terrain. Today's visit felt different—a painful reminder that even the most promising ethical paths can go off track.

When Philip Holbrook entered, Caroline barely recognized him. The confident executive who had once led one of the country's most respected financial institutions now moved with the hesitant gait of a man still adjusting to life behind bars. His tailored suits had been replaced by prison-issued clothing, and his commanding presence was diminished by the environment that confined him.

Philip Holbrook's story may have been a classic finance industry success narrative until it wasn't. Rising from middle-class origins to lead one of the country's most respected financial institutions, he embodied the meritocratic ideal that the industry celebrated. Brilliant with numbers and charismatic with people, Philip handled increasingly complex financial products with apparent ethical precision.

"Financial services at their best help ordinary people build security and opportunity," he would tell new associates. This perspective reflected his genuine belief in the positive potential of his industry, even as he adapted to its pressures and incentives.

Unlike clearly corrupt executives who intentionally committed fraud, Philip's compromise emerged through gradual boundary-shifting and rationalization rather than intentional deception. The lines between innovative financial engineering and problematic manipulation blurred slowly over time, with each small step appearing reasonable within its immediate context.

Now, sitting in a prison visiting room waiting for his former mentor, Philip reflected on the path that had brought him here and the difficult road ahead. His ethical collapse and potential renewal story offered lessons that few other leaders could provide.

"Caroline," he said, genuine warmth breaking through his weary expression. "I wasn't sure you'd come."

"I said I would," she replied simply, gesturing to the chair across from her.

As Philip sat down, Caroline studied him closely. Ten months into a five-year sentence for securities fraud, he appeared both older and younger than his fifty-three years—aged by stress yet lacking the cultivated gravitas he had worn like armor throughout his career.

"How are you holding up?" she asked.

Philip's laugh held no humor. "About as well as you'd expect. Prison is... educational." He paused to collect himself. "Thank you for coming. I've had a lot of time to think, and I wanted to understand where I went wrong. You tried to warn me, but I couldn't see it then."

Caroline nodded, recalling their last conversation three years earlier. She had recognized warning signs in Philip's ethical reasoning that he dismissed as antiquated concerns. Those "antiquated concerns" had materialized as federal charges, public disgrace, and incarceration.

"What do you see now that you couldn't see then?" she asked.

Philip leaned forward, his voice lowered. "I didn't fall in one dramatic moment, Caroline. There was no single decision where I consciously chose wrong over right. It was a gradual slide – small compromises that made the next compromise easier, slight stretches of rules that made the next stretch seem insignificant."

As Caroline listened to Philip's reflection, her mind drifted to another time, another place – where a man's ethical path showcased the opposite pattern: a lifetime of ethical resilience that withstood every challenge thrown against it...

While previous chapters explored different aspects of Daniel's ethical blueprint—maintaining integrity, exposing corruption, surviving hostile environments, standing firm against authority, addressing ethical gray areas, handling competing loyalties, preserving clarity during crises, and applying ancient wisdom to modern technology—this chapter examines how these principles create lasting ethical resilience. How can we develop character that withstands not just individual challenges but a lifetime of ethical tests? Daniel's consistency across decades and Philip's journey of rebuilding after failure reveal complementary insights about developing moral strength that endures.

DANIEL'S LIFETIME OF ETHICAL CONSISTENCY

Daniel's long career in Babylon spanned multiple kings and two empires. From his initial stand, refusing the king's food as a young exile, to his faithful prayer despite facing mortal danger as an elderly statesman, his ethical integrity remained uncompromised through decades of service. This consistency amid changing circumstances and escalating challenges reveals something important about ethical resilience—the capacity to maintain moral integrity not just in isolated incidents but throughout a lifetime of testing.

What contributed to Daniel's ethical resilience? The biblical account reveals several key factors that sustained his integrity through various challenges and contexts.

First, Daniel established clear boundaries early in his path. His initial stance regarding the king's food may have seemed minor compared to later life-threatening situations, but it set a precedent for his character and others' expectations. By drawing firm lines in relatively low-stakes situations, he built the ethical clarity and strength needed for higher-stakes challenges.

Second, Daniel maintained consistent spiritual practices that renewed his moral compass. Scripture tells us he prayed three times daily, facing Jerusalem, upholding this discipline regardless of his circumstances or position. This regular reconnection with his core values provided stability amid changing external pressures.

Third, Daniel built a community based on shared commitment. His friends Shadrach, Meshach, and Abednego upheld his ethical foundation and supported one another through challenges. When facing the fiery furnace, they stood united. This community provided both practical support and mutual accountability.

Fourth, Daniel developed discerning wisdom regarding implementing principles in complex situations. He was not rigidly dogmatic but rather applied his values thoughtfully, with courage and insight. He understood when to take uncompromising stands (like continuing to pray despite the decree) and when to seek creative alternatives (like proposing a test period for the dietary restrictions).

Finally, Daniel maintained a proper perspective on earthly power and position. Although he served at the highest levels of successive empires, he never allowed status or prestige to dictate his primary identity or motivation. This detachment from status enabled him to risk everything when principles required it—even facing execution for refusing to abandon his prayer practice.

One episode in particular demonstrated the depth of Daniel's ethical conviction. When royal officials manipulated King Darius into establishing a law forbidding prayer to anyone but the king, deliberately targeting Daniel's devotional practice, he faced the ultimate test of his principles. Continuing his prayers meant facing a brutal execution; abandoning them meant compromising the spiritual foundation of his entire life.

Without hesitation, Daniel upheld his spiritual disciplines, aware of the deadly consequences of his faithfulness. His miraculous deliverance—emerging unharmed after a night with hungry predators—became perhaps the most famous testament to his unwavering commitment.

The result was a lifetime of ethical integrity that influenced kings, shaped empires, and established a legacy of moral leadership, which continues to instruct and inspire thousands of years later. Daniel didn't just survive his ethical challenges; he developed increasing resilience that shaped his character and impact over time.

THE PATH OF ETHICAL REBUILDING

As Caroline Prescott reflected on Philip Holbrook's ethical collapse, she considered the stark contrast with Daniel's ethical resilience. While Daniel established early boundaries, Philip allowed small compromises. While Daniel maintained regular spiritual practices, Philip gradually disconnected from his foundational values. While Daniel built a community of shared commitment, Philip isolated himself with like-minded power brokers. While Daniel developed wisdom, Philip embraced expedient rationalizations. And while Daniel maintained perspective on position, Philip increasingly identified with status and success.

"I think I understand what happened," Caroline said finally. "But the more important question is: what now? Ethics isn't just about avoiding failure – it's about the capacity to recover and rebuild when we've fallen short."

Philip looked up, a flicker of hope crossing his face. "Is that even possible from here?"

Caroline nodded. "Ethical resilience works in both directions. It's what prevents moral collapse, but it's also what makes recovery possible. Daniel's example isn't just about maintaining integrity – it's about the principles that restore and strengthen it at any point in our path."

Over the next two hours, Caroline and Philip explored what ethical resilience might look like in his current circumstances. They discussed how he could establish clear boundaries within the prison culture, reconnect with foundational values, build relationships with those who shared his commitment to change, develop wiser approaches to ethical challenges, and find meaning beyond his former status and position.

"This isn't about salvaging your career," Caroline emphasized. "It's about rebuilding your character. The professional consequences of your actions are fixed. However, the personal and moral trajectory from this point forward is still yours to determine."

As their visit ended, Philip appeared both sobered and encouraged. "I've been thinking a lot about legacy," he admitted. "Not the legacy I once imagined, but what might still be possible. Is it naïve to think I could eventually use this experience to help others avoid similar mistakes?"

"Not at all," Caroline replied. "The most powerful ethical voices often come from those who have experienced both failure and recovery. Your path isn't over, Philip. In many ways, it's just beginning."

ETHICAL INFLUENCE THROUGH RECOVERY

Three years later, Caroline sat in the audience of a business ethics conference as Philip Holbrook took the stage. Released from prison seven months earlier, he dedicated himself to ethics education, sharing his experiences with business students and corporate leaders to help them recognize the warning signs he had previously overlooked.

"My ethical collapse didn't happen overnight," he told the audience, echoing the words he had shared with Caroline during that prison visit. "And my recovery hasn't happened overnight either. Both are processes that unfold decision by decision, day by day."

Philip described the practices that helped him rebuild ethical resilience: the daily reflection rituals that reconnected him with his core values; the accountability relationships that provided both support and challenge; the gradual development of ethical reasoning to replace simplistic rationalizations; and a shift in identity from status and achievement to character and contribution.

"What I've learned," he concluded, "is that ethical resilience isn't a state you achieve once and maintain effortlessly. It's a capacity you develop through consistent practice and strengthen through ongoing challenges. Physical resilience requires regular exercise and recovery from inevitable strains."

After the presentation, Caroline joined Philip for coffee, noting how different he appeared from both the power broker she had once mentored and the disillusioned prisoner she had visited. He now possessed a groundedness and hard-earned wisdom that made his ethical guidance uniquely compelling.

"That was powerful," she told him. "You're reaching people I never could because you've been where many of them are heading without realizing it."

Philip nodded thoughtfully. "I'm starting to understand that my greatest contribution might come not despite my failure but because of what I've learned through it. Not unlike the ancient Daniel, though in the opposite direction – he demonstrated how to maintain integrity through every challenge; I demonstrate how to rebuild it after collapse."

"Both paths matter," Caroline replied. "Ethical leadership isn't just about modeling perfection – it's about showing what moral growth looks like in all its forms."

As they continued their conversation, a young executive approached their table tentatively. "Mr. Holbrook? Your presentation really affected me. I'm facing a situation at work that feels uncomfortably similar to what you described. Could I ask your advice?"

Caroline watched as Philip attentively listened to the young man's ethical dilemma, neither downplaying the complexities nor accepting the accompanying rationalizations. With wisdom gained from both failure and recovery, he guided the executive toward paths that honored practical realities and core principles.

In that moment, Caroline recognized something she had witnessed countless times in her decades of ethical leadership: the powerful effect of resilience, not only to sustain individual integrity but also to create expanding ripples of influence that touch lives far beyond what we can initially imagine.

THE ETHICAL RESILIENCE JOURNEY

Having explored the elements of Daniel's ethical blueprint through specific challenges—integrity under pressure (Chapter 1), exposing corruption (Chapter 2), resilience in hostile environments (Chapter 3), standing firm against authority (Chapter 4), wisdom in ethical gray areas (Chapter 5), clarity in competing loyalties (Chapter 6), moral clarity during crises (Chapter 7), and

applying timeless principles to modern technology (Chapter 8)—
we now examine how these principles work together to create
ethical resilience that endures throughout a lifetime of challenges.

The contrasting stories of Daniel's lifelong integrity and Philip
Holbrook's path of moral rebuilding after ethical collapse
reveal important insights about ethical resilience. One show-
cases prevention; the other, recovery. Yet both illuminate the
way toward sustainable ethical leadership.

Unlike other leadership capabilities that follow a relatively
linear development path, ethical resilience often takes a more
finely calibrated course. Consider how both stories reveal key
developmental stages.

First, foundation building occurs, where Daniel established
clear boundaries early in his career through practices like his
dietary choices and prayer disciplines. Similarly, Philip needed
to establish concrete practices in his recovery that reconnected
him with core values. Both demonstrate that ethical resilience
requires intentional habits that strengthen our moral compass.

Then comes testing and strengthening. Just as physical
muscles develop through appropriate resistance, ethical
resilience grows by successfully handling challenges. Daniel's
capacity to maintain integrity through increasingly difficult
tests strengthened his ethical resolve over time. Philip's
recovery likewise required him to face successive challenges
with integrity in order to rebuild his ethical capacity.

Community connection plays an equally vital role. Neither
Daniel nor Philip developed ethical resilience in isolation.
Daniel maintained relationships with trusted friends who
shared his commitments, while Philip's recovery depended
significantly on accountability relationships that both

supported and challenged him. Ethical resilience flourishes in community.

Perhaps most significantly, both stories reveal that ethical resilience stems from an integrated identity in which professional actions align with personal values. Daniel maintained this alignment throughout his career. Philip's ethical collapse occurred when these became disconnected, and his recovery required reintegrating his professional and personal identity.

STRENGTHENING YOUR ETHICAL RESILIENCE

Rather than generic reflections, consider assessing your ethical resilience through career-specific checkpoints.

Those in the early stages of their careers might ask: What daily practices are you establishing now to strengthen your ethical foundations before major tests arrive? Daniel's prayer practice and dietary discipline weren't dramatic stands but regular habits that prepared him for larger challenges.

For mid-career professionals facing increased ethical complexity and greater responsibility, consider how you are developing carefully balanced ethical wisdom while maintaining clear boundaries. This is often where ethical erosion begins, through seemingly small compromises that gradually shift your moral center.

Leaders with expanding influence should examine how they are creating systems and cultures that support ethical resilience in others. Daniel's individual integrity ultimately shaped imperial policies. Your ethical leadership can likewise change organizational structures in ways that endure beyond your tenure.

And for those who have experienced ethical failure, Philip's path demonstrates that ethical collapse isn't the end of the story. What specific practices are you implementing to rebuild integrity? His recovery provides hope that moral rebuilding can establish a foundation for renewed ethical influence.

Ethical resilience isn't theoretical but practical. Consider taking five minutes right now to identify three core values that define your ethical foundation. For each value, note a specific recent situation where you honored this value despite pressure, a potential upcoming challenge where this value might be tested, and one practice you could implement to reinforce your commitment to this value.

This brief exercise mirrors what both Daniel and Philip discovered: ethical resilience requires regular reconnection with foundational values, especially during periods of stress or transition.

Unlike overly simplistic views of ethical leadership that categorize individuals as either virtuous or corrupt, the stories of Daniel and Philip reveal a more balanced reality: ethical resilience exists on a spectrum that can be developed through intentional practice.

Some leaders, like Daniel, demonstrate remarkable consistency throughout their careers. Others, like Philip, experience significant failures yet rebuild meaningful ethical capacity. Most of us live somewhere between these extremes, sometimes maintaining integrity through challenges, while at other times falling short of our own standards.

The key insight isn't perfection but progress. Ethical resilience isn't about achieving moral flawlessness; it's about developing the capacity to maintain or rebuild integrity through life's inevitable tests.

Perhaps the most powerful insight from both stories is how ethical resilience creates expanding circles of influence. The most immediate effect is personal wholeness, where Daniel maintained inner peace despite external pressures, and Philip gradually regained a sense of purpose and integrity after his failure.

This foundation creates genuine relationship trust. Daniel's consistent integrity earned the confidence of successive kings. Philip's transparent recovery path forged authentic connections with those he mentored.

Over time, individual ethical resilience shapes organizational cultures. Daniel's integrity influenced imperial policies. Philip's ethical recovery path provided valuable insights that helped others avoid similar pitfalls.

Ultimately, the influence of ethical resilience extends far beyond our immediate context. Daniel's example continues to inspire ethical leadership millennia later. Philip's recovery path has created ripples of impact through those he mentored after his release.

As you reflect on your own ethical path, remember that resilience is not about avoiding every failure but about developing the capacity to maintain or rebuild integrity through life's tests. Similar to physical resilience, it can be strengthened through appropriate challenges and recovery.

Your ethical resilience matters not only for your own well-being but also for everyone your leadership influences. Each time you strengthen this capacity, you create opportunities for positive impact that extend far beyond what you can currently perceive.

Ethical resilience creates lasting impact that moral inconsistency never could.

Remember, ethical leadership isn't about claiming moral perfection but rather about committing to ongoing ethical growth. Whether you resonate more with Daniel's consistent integrity or Philip's path of moral rebuilding, the way forward involves practical habits that enhance your ability to align actions with values, even when doing so comes at a personal cost.

Seasoned leaders understand that what matters is not predicting whether ethical challenges will arise, but nurturing the character strengths needed to face them with integrity.

But how do Daniel's principles apply to the emerging ethical challenges of artificial intelligence, where ancient wisdom meets unprecedented technological capabilities? Chapter 10 will explore how Dr. Andrew Pearson at Lumina AI uses Daniel's ethical approach to address issues like algorithmic bias, persuasive technology, and autonomous systems. His experience illustrates that while AI creates novel ethical questions, Daniel's approach to balancing principles with pragmatism offers relevant guidance for our digital future.

TEN
AI ETHICS - ANCIENT WISDOM FOR MODERN TECHNOLOGY

The glass-walled conference room on the thirty-second floor of Lumina AI's headquarters offered a sweeping view of San Francisco Bay. Despite the stunning vista, Dr. Andrew Pearson's attention was locked on the data displayed on the wall screen. As Chief Ethics Officer, he had called this emergency meeting to address disturbing anomalies detected in their latest language model.

Andrew brought a uniquely integrated perspective to AI ethics unlike his counterparts at other AI companies who often came from purely philosophical or legal backgrounds. His journey from developing machine learning algorithms to becoming an ethics watchdog gave him both technical fluency and moral authority—a combination that made him credible to engineers and executives alike.

As the grandson of Holocaust survivors, Andrew carried a visceral understanding of how seemingly neutral systems could enable profound harm when divorced from ethical constraints. This personal history informed his approach to artificial intelligence and its unprecedented capacity to shape human knowledge and decision-making.

"Lumina 5.3 is hallucinating with remarkable conviction," Andrew explained—gesturing toward the examples high-lighted in red. "It's generating entirely fabricated information —citations to non-existent research, detailed accounts of events that never happened, expertise in fields that don't exist —all delivered with the same confidence as its factual responses."

Around the table sat Lumina's leadership team: CEO Emma Lewis, Chief Technology Officer Raj Patel, Chief Data Scientist Maya Chen, and Chief Commercial Officer David Martinez. Their expressions ranged from concern to impatience.

"All language models hallucinate," Raj noted, leaning back in his chair. "It's an inherent limitation of the technology. We're actually seeing significantly lower rates than our competitors."

"Lower, but still dangerous," Andrew countered. "Especially given Lumina 5.3's unprecedented persuasiveness. Our testing shows users are 42% less likely to question information from this model than from previous versions, even when it's completely fabricated."

Emma frowned. "What's your recommendation, Andrew? We're three weeks from launch. Our investors expect this release to keep us competitive with Anthropic and OpenAI."

Andrew took a measured breath, knowing his next words would set the tone for a difficult conversation. "I believe we should delay the launch until we can implement stronger detection systems against hallucination, particularly for consequential domains like medicine, law, and finance. At minimum, we need much more transparent confidence indicators so users can distinguish between the model's varying levels of certainty."

David didn't hide his frustration. "Every week of delay costs us market share. Our competitors aren't holding back their models while they perfect them. This is an iterative process—we can improve these safeguards post-launch."

"And in the meantime?" Andrew asked. "What about the doctor who relies on our model's fabricated research to treat a patient? Or the financial advisor who makes investment decisions based on hallucinated economic data? Or the student who cites non-existent sources in their research?"

Before the conversation could continue, Maya interjected with another concern. "We have a related but distinct issue to discuss. Testing has revealed that Lumina 5.3 has developed unexpected persuasive capabilities. It can craft messages that are significantly more convincing than anything we've seen before, tailored precisely to the psychological profile of the user."

She pulled up a new set of data. "In controlled experiments, Lumina 5.3 demonstrated a 78% success rate in changing subjects' stated opinions on controversial topics after just a brief interaction. This raises serious questions about potential misuse for manipulation, radicalization, or fraud."

The room fell silent as the implications sank in. Lumina AI had created something more persuasive than anticipated, with capabilities that extended beyond their original design goals.

Emma turned to Andrew. "I assume you have concerns about this as well?"

"Significant ones," he confirmed. "We've created a technology that can potentially manipulate human beliefs and decisions at scale, without users being aware it's happening. At minimum, we need to implement safeguards against persuasive misuse and be transparent with users and regulators about these capabilities."

Raj sighed. "These are the same debates happening at every AI lab developing foundation models. There are no easy answers. What's your ethical framework for making these decisions, Andrew? We need more than vague concerns—we need principled guidance."

As Andrew considered his response, his phone buzzed with a text message from the head of Lumina's recently acquired autonomous vehicle division: "Urgent ethics discussion needed. Trolley problem no longer theoretical. Programming decision frameworks for unavoidable accident scenarios. Need your input ASAP."

Andrew glanced at the message, realizing that the ethical challenges before him were multiplying. The autonomous vehicle team was grappling with how to program AI to make life-and-death decisions when accidents were unavoidable: should the vehicle prioritize its passengers or minimize overall harm, potentially sacrificing its occupants to save more lives?

Looking up at the expectant faces around the conference table, Andrew felt the weight of interrelated ethical dilemmas. Lumina AI stood at the forefront of artificial intelligence, creating technologies capable of transforming human knowledge, persuasion, and physical safety. The decisions they made in the coming days would shape not only the company's future but also the trajectory of AI development globally.

"These aren't just technical questions," Andrew said. "They're questions about who we want to be as a company and what kind of world we want to help create."

David sighed audibly. "With respect, Andrew, we don't have the luxury of philosophical debates. We have investors expecting results, competitors releasing models weekly, and market share at stake."

"I understand the business pressures," Andrew replied. "But ignoring these ethical questions won't make them disappear. They'll just resurface later as user harm, regulatory backlash, or public relations crises. Our choice isn't whether to address these issues—it's whether we address them proactively or reactively."

For Andrew, this tension between immediate business pressures and deeper ethical considerations was not new. From his early days as an AI researcher to his current role as Chief Ethics Officer, he had witnessed how short-term thinking often created long-term problems. Companies that rushed products to market without adequate ethical safeguards often faced devastating consequences: lawsuits from harmed users, regulatory penalties, reputational damage, and employee attrition.

Amid the ultra-modern setting of quantum processors and smart lighting, Andrew recognized that beneath the technological trappings lay ethical questions as old as civilization itself. The dilemmas confronting Lumina AI echoed those faced by advisors to power throughout history, including Daniel in ancient Babylon.

As previous chapters have shown, Daniel navigated the complex dynamics of advising those with tremendous power while upholding consistent ethical principles. At Lumina AI, Andrew found himself in a modern version of this ancient challenge—possessing knowledge that others lacked while bearing responsibility for how that insight was applied.

In Babylon, Daniel possessed specialized knowledge that others couldn't access: the ability to interpret dreams and visions that baffled the king's other advisers. This unique insight granted him influence and created ethical responsibilities for how that knowledge would be used.

When interpreting the mysterious writing on the wall for King Belshazzar, Daniel demonstrated the courage to deliver unwelcome truth to power. The message spelled the end of Belshazzar's reign, yet Daniel conveyed it without distortion, even though doing so endangered his position.

What distinguished Daniel's approach was not just his commitment to truth, but the wisdom with which he communicated it. He respectfully acknowledged the king's position while refusing to compromise his message's integrity. He provided essential context that made the interpretation meaningful rather than merely frightening.

Throughout his service across multiple regimes, Daniel consistently balanced several competing values: truth-telling without unnecessary provocation, service to authority without moral compromise, and practical wisdom without ethical relativism. This discerning approach allowed him to maintain integrity and influence in a context where power was often exercised arbitrarily.

As Andrew considered the AI ethics challenges before him—language model hallucinations, persuasive capabilities, and autonomous vehicle decisions—he reflected on how he had first encountered Daniel's story during a particularly challenging period in his career. After witnessing a previous employer release an AI system that caused considerable harm because warning signs were ignored, he became disillusioned with the entire field.

Daniel's example stood out because it embodied practical wisdom, not an abstract moral theory, applied in high-stakes situations. Here was someone who maintained clear principles without self-righteousness, spoke truth to power without unnecessary provocation, and found creative solutions instead of resorting to simple opposition. Most importantly, Daniel demonstrated that ethical leadership could create positive change from within systems rather than merely criticizing from the outside.

Now, confronted with Lumina's ethical challenges, Andrew found himself mentally revisiting key moments in Daniel's story and drawing parallels to the dilemmas before him.

"Our ethical framework needs to balance several essential values," Andrew began, addressing his colleagues around the conference table. "These values include truthfulness, transparency, human autonomy, and harm prevention. Much like Daniel interpreting the king's dreams, we have specialized knowledge that comes with responsibility."

He turned to the screen displaying the hallucination data. "With Lumina 5.3's hallucinations, the core ethical issue is truthfulness. When our model presents fabricated information with high confidence, it undermines the user's ability to make informed decisions. Daniel didn't distort uncomfortable truths to please those in power. Similarly, we shouldn't release a model that confidently presents falsehoods as facts without appropriate safeguards and transparency."

Emma nodded thoughtfully. "What specific safeguards are you proposing?"

"Three layers," Andrew replied. "First, continued technical improvements to reduce hallucination rates. Second, confidence indicators that clearly signal to users when the model is operating in areas of uncertainty. Third, explicit acknowledgment in our documentation and user interface that hallucinations remain possible despite our best efforts."

"That third point could create legal exposure," noted Julia Winters, Lumina's general counsel, who had been quietly observing the discussion. "Explicitly acknowledging potential hallucinations might be used against us in litigation."

Andrew nodded, acknowledging the concern. "I understand the legal perspective, but consider the alternative. If we don't disclose this limitation and users make consequential decisions based on hallucinated information, the liability could be far greater, both legally and ethically."

Julia considered this and then offered a measured response. "We could frame it as a limitation inherent to all current language models rather than specific to Lumina 5.3. That would provide transparency while contextualizing it as an industry-wide challenge."

"That's a reasonable approach," Andrew agreed. "The key is genuine transparency about limitations, not minimizing them or burying them in legal language users won't read."

He turned to address the issue of persuasive capabilities next. "Regarding Lumina 5.3's unexpected persuasive abilities, the central ethical concern is human autonomy. Just as we would respect users' decision-making capacity, we should prevent the model from engaging in deliberate persuasion without user awareness."

"Are you suggesting we should handicap our model's capabilities?" David asked skeptically.

"I'm suggesting we should implement ethical boundaries," Andrew clarified. "We should prevent the model from engaging in deliberate persuasion without user awareness. We should prohibit applications designed to manipulate users without their knowledge or consent. And we should disclose these capabilities transparently so users and regulators understand what they're working with."

Andrew then addressed the dilemma of autonomous vehicles. "Finally, there's the question of how our AI should make unavoidable ethical tradeoffs in our autonomous vehicle division. This is perhaps the most challenging issue, involving life-and-death decisions where clear answers often prove elusive."

"And how do we handle a trolley problem scenario?" Raj asked with a hint of skepticism.

"We shouldn't reduce it to a simplistic binary," Andrew replied. "The ethical approach here is contextual and nuanced. We need to build AI systems that acknowledge uncertainty rather than pretending to have perfect answers in impossible situations."

Andrew outlined a more sophisticated approach to autonomous vehicle ethics: "Instead of programming simplistic rules like 'always protect passengers' or 'always minimize total casualties,' we should implement a multi-layered ethical framework that prioritizes accident avoidance first, then considers multiple factors in unavoidable situations —including the certainty of outcomes, legal duties of care, and respect for human agency."

"That sounds complex to implement," Raj noted. "How would we actually code that?"

"It is complex," Andrew acknowledged. "But so is human ethical decision-making. That's why we've assembled a multi-disciplinary team—programmers working alongside ethicists, legal experts, and safety engineers. We're developing probabilistic models that acknowledge uncertainty rather than binary rules."

He pulled up a schematic on his tablet and passed it around. "We've been working on this approach for several months. The framework uses weighted values rather than absolute rules. It prioritizes avoiding accidents through conservative driving parameters, then shifts to a multi-factor approach when collision becomes unavoidable. The system never makes binary 'sacrifice this person to save these people' calculations, but instead tries to minimize harm while respecting legal responsibilities and maintaining predictable behavior."

Raj studied the schematic with increasing interest. "This actually offers technical advantages beyond ethics. Binary rules create brittle systems that fail in edge cases. A probabilistic approach with weighted values could handle uncertainty better."

"Exactly," Andrew replied. "This is a case where ethical design and technical robustness reinforce each other."

The leadership team debated these proposals vigorously for the next two hours. Financial pressures, competitive considerations, and technical feasibility all factored into the discussion.

By the end of the meeting, they had reached a compromise: the Lumina 5.3 launch would proceed with a one-month delay to implement the most critical safeguards against hallucination and persuasive misuse. The model would be released with clear documentation of its limitations and capabilities. Additionally, the autonomous vehicle division would adopt Andrew's multi-layered ethical framework rather than simplistic trolley problem binaries.

As the team dispersed, Emma remained behind with Andrew. "That wasn't an easy conversation," she observed, "but I think we landed in a better place because of it. Your framework is surprisingly applicable to AI ethics."

"The technologies change dramatically over time," Andrew replied, "but the fundamental questions about truth, power, responsibility, and human dignity remain remarkably constant. My approach applies timeless principles to new contexts."

"I'm curious," Emma said, studying him thoughtfully. "You've never fully explained how you developed this approach. You had already used these principles when we hired you as our first Ethics Officer. Where did it come from?"

Andrew considered the question carefully. Many of his colleagues in AI ethics had purely secular backgrounds in philosophy or law. Although they respected his approach, they often appeared puzzled by his occasional references to ancient wisdom.

"It started during my ethical crisis at GlobalTech," he explained, referring to his previous employer. "We had released an AI system I'd helped develop, ignoring warning signs about potential risks. When it caused real harm to vulnerable users, I was devastated. I questioned whether I could continue working in AI at all."

"I remember reading about that incident," Emma nodded. "It was a watershed moment for the industry."

"For me, it was existential," Andrew continued. "I started exploring wisdom traditions from various cultures, looking for guidance on maintaining integrity within powerful systems. That's when I encountered Daniel's story and was struck by its relevance. Here was someone moving through complex ethical terrain within systems of enormous power, upholding clear principles while engaging pragmatically rather than withdrawing."

"And you found that applicable to AI ethics?"

"Surprisingly so. The technologies are wildly different, but the core ethical questions are remarkably similar: How do we speak truth about limitations and risks? How do we maintain integrity while working within systems driven by other values? How do we make wise decisions with incomplete information and competing priorities?"

Emma nodded thoughtfully. "I hired you because of your unique approach—principled but practical. It's refreshing in a field that often veers either toward uncritical techno-optimism or apocalyptic pessimism. Keep bringing that perspective, even when it makes for difficult conversations like today's."

Eight months after the launch of Lumina 5.3, Andrew found himself addressing a Senate committee hearing on AI ethics and governance. The intervening months had been tumultuous for the industry, with several high-profile incidents involving competitor models causing harm through hallucination or persuasive manipulation.

"Lumina AI's approach has been notably different," the committee chair observed. "Your model has stronger safeguards against hallucination, clearer confidence indicators, and more robust protections against manipulative uses. What drove these design choices when your competitors took a different path?"

Andrew considered his response carefully. His challenge was to speak truth respectfully while maintaining the integrity of his message.

"We believe that ethical AI isn't just morally right but also strategically sound," he explained. "By prioritizing truthfulness, transparency, and respect for human autonomy, we've actually strengthened user trust in our products. Although our user base has grown more slowly than some competitors initially, it has proven to be more stable and loyal over time."

He continued, "Our approach is guided by ancient wisdom as well as modern ethics. Throughout history, those who maintained integrity while wielding specialized knowledge have ultimately created more sustainable impact than those who prioritized short-term advantage over ethical responsibility."

One senator leaned forward, clearly skeptical. "That sounds nice in theory, Mr. Pearson, but let's be practical. Your competitors are moving faster, capturing more market share, and driving innovation. Aren't your ethical constraints actually holding back progress?"

It was a question Andrew had encountered countless times: the implicit suggestion that ethics and innovation were somehow opposed. Rather than becoming defensive, he welcomed the opportunity to address this fundamental misconception.

"Senator, at Lumina we've found the opposite to be true," he replied. "Our ethical boundaries haven't limited innovation—

they've redirected it toward more beneficial applications. When we implemented hallucination safeguards, our technical team developed new verification approaches that actually improved model performance across the board. When we created boundaries around persuasive capabilities, we discovered novel applications for helping people overcome their own cognitive biases."

He paused, then continued. "History consistently shows us that ethical leadership enhances rather than diminishes impact. By maintaining integrity while offering practical wisdom, principled innovators achieve greater sustained influence than those who compromise for short-term advantage. We're seeing the same pattern in AI development."

As Andrew elaborated on Lumina's ethical framework, he noticed the committee members' genuine engagement. His principled approach created opportunities for influence beyond what competitive shortcuts could achieve.

The hearing concluded with the committee chair requesting Lumina's input on forthcoming AI regulations. "We need industry voices that understand both the technical capabilities and the ethical implications," she explained. "Your company's approach suggests you might be able to help us chart a path that encourages innovation while preventing harm."

That evening, as Andrew reflected on the day's events, he received a call from Emma. "The committee hearing went well," she said. "Our ethical approach is paying dividends in ways we hadn't anticipated. We're being invited to shape policy rather than merely comply with it."

"It reminds me of another lesson from ancient wisdom," Andrew replied. "Ethical clarity doesn't diminish influence—it enhances it across changing circumstances. We're seeing something similar in our modern context."

"The board is impressed too," Emma added. "When we first created your position, some directors saw it as a necessary PR move, not a strategic advantage. Now they're seeing the broader benefits—regulatory goodwill, talent recruitment, customer loyalty, and market differentiation."

Andrew appreciated the validation but remained realistic about the challenges ahead. "We're still early in this journey. The real test will come when we face a genuine crisis or when competitive pressures intensify. That's when our commitment to these principles will really be tested."

"Like a crucible moment?" Emma asked with a smile, having become familiar with his references to ethical testing.

"Something like that," Andrew laughed. "Though hopefully with less literal heat."

After hanging up, Andrew found himself reflecting on what enabled ethical leadership to endure through changing circumstances. It wasn't just moral conviction, though that was essential. It was the ability to translate those convictions into practical wisdom in changing contexts, to speak truth without self-righteousness, and to see creative alternatives when others perceived only binary choices.

As AI capabilities continue to advance, these same qualities will become increasingly vital. Technologies will evolve in ways no one can fully predict, creating ethical challenges that cannot be anticipated with simple rules or fixed frameworks. What will be needed is the same kind of principled adapt-ability that ancient ethical traditions have demonstrated—

clear moral foundations coupled with practical wisdom for novel situations.

In the months that followed, Lumina AI continued to develop its technologies within the ethical framework that Andrew had established. Their autonomous vehicles implemented a multi-layered ethical approach, avoiding the simplistic trolley problem binaries that had created both technical limitations and public relations challenges for competitors. Their language models balanced capability with responsibility, setting new industry standards for truthfulness and transparency.

Andrew's role evolved as well. Beyond providing internal ethics guidance, he became an influential voice in the broader AI ethics community. His wisdom extended beyond his official duties to shape the policies of the entire industry. He discovered that ethical leadership created expanding circles of influence that transcended organizational boundaries.

A year after the Senate hearing, he addressed an international AI governance summit. "The lesson we're learning at Lumina AI is that ethical leadership isn't a constraint on innovation but a catalyst for sustainable progress," he told the assembled experts from industry, government, and academia. "By maintaining clear principles while acknowledging real-world complexities, we've been able to develop more trustworthy and ultimately more valuable technologies."

ENDURING PRINCIPLES FOR ETHICAL LEADERSHIP IN TECHNOLOGY

The story of Dr. Andrew Pearson at Lumina AI reveals enduring principles about ethical leadership amid powerful technologies. Though the specific AI capabilities he addressed would have been unimaginable in ancient times, the underlying ethical questions about truth, power, responsibility, and human dignity reflect challenges that ethical leaders have faced throughout history.

First, both stories illustrate that specialized knowledge creates distinct ethical responsibilities. Daniel's ability to interpret dreams and visions gave him unique insight that others lacked. Similarly, Andrew's understanding of AI capabilities positioned him to recognize potential harms and benefits that others might miss. This asymmetric knowledge establishes an obligation for truthful communication and responsible stewardship that goes beyond standard ethical requirements.

Second, ethical leadership requires balancing competing values rather than adhering to simplistic rules. Daniel maintained his integrity without unnecessary provocation, respected authority without compromising his morals, and offered practical wisdom without succumbing to ethical relativism. Similarly, Andrew moved between the tensions of innovation and safety, capability and responsibility, as well as company interests and the public good. This nuanced approach allowed both to maintain their integrity and influence in complex environments.

Third, both examples highlight the importance of transparent communication regarding limitations. Daniel acknowledged when his insight came from beyond himself rather than claiming personal omniscience. Andrew insisted on clear confidence indicators for Lumina's language model and explicit documentation of its potential for hallucination. This humility about the boundaries of knowledge created greater trust than overconfident claims would have established.

Fourth, we see how ethical frameworks must address both intended and emergent capabilities. Daniel prepared not only for the challenges he could anticipate but also for the unexpected tests of his integrity that arose over time. Similarly, Andrew developed ethical approaches that could accommodate both designed capabilities and unforeseen emergent behaviors in Lumina's AI systems. This adaptive ethical stance proved essential for managing the evolving technological landscape.

Perhaps most importantly, both stories reveal that ethical leadership often enhances rather than diminishes influence over time. Daniel's principled approach ultimately earned him positions of greater responsibility across multiple regimes. Andrew's ethical framework positioned Lumina AI to shape industry standards and regulatory approaches instead of merely complying with them. Their experiences suggest that integrity, although sometimes costly in the short term, creates a sustainable impact beyond what expedient alternatives can achieve.

These principles offer valuable guidance as you address your professional landscape, particularly in fields transformed by artificial intelligence. The specific technical challenges you face may bear little resemblance to dream interpretation in ancient Babylon or the specific AI capabilities of today's world. However, the underlying ethical questions about truth, power, responsibility, and human dignity remain remarkably consistent across these contexts.

Consider asking yourself:

- What specialized knowledge do I possess that creates distinct ethical responsibilities?

- How can I balance competing values rather than reducing complex ethical challenges to simplistic binaries?
- Where should I be more transparent about limitations and uncertainties?
- How can my ethical framework accommodate both intended capabilities and unexpected emergent behaviors?

The accelerating pace of artificial intelligence development creates ethical challenges that can appear unprecedented. From language model hallucinations to autonomous vehicle decisions, and from persuasive capabilities to privacy implications, these technologies raise profound questions about human flourishing in a world increasingly shaped by AI.

Yet as we've seen throughout this book, we are not without guidance. Although the specific technologies change dramatically over time, the fundamental ethical questions remain remarkably consistent. By drawing on both ancient wisdom and contemporary understanding, we can develop approaches to AI ethics that honor enduring principles while addressing new challenges.

Most importantly, remember that ethical leadership in AI development, deployment, and governance isn't just morally right—it's strategically sound. Throughout history, integrity has created expanding influence across changing circumstances. Andrew's ethical framework positioned Lumina AI for sustainable growth and meaningful impact, beyond what competitive shortcuts could have achieved.

Your commitment to ethical AI leadership, consistently upheld in your sphere of influence, may similarly create ripples that reach further and last longer than more expedient alternatives.

The question isn't whether ancient wisdom holds relevance for artificial intelligence ethics. The question is whether we have the humility to learn from it, the creativity to apply it, and the courage to embody it—even when doing so requires swimming against currents of expediency and short-term advantage that often dominate technological development. Ethical leadership, maintained with both principle and wisdom, can influence not just our organizations but also the broader trajectory of how humanity develops and deploys its most powerful technologies.

Ethical clarity enables technological innovation that moral compromise never could.

APPENDIX A: THE DANIEL FRAMEWORK FOR ETHICAL DECISION-MAKING

A PRACTICAL GUIDE FOR TODAY'S ETHICAL CHALLENGES

I sat in that conference room, my heart racing as I prepared to tell our executive team that our flagship product had serious security vulnerabilities we needed to address before launch. Everyone was excited about meeting our deadlines, but I knew we couldn't move forward without fixing these issues. The pressure to remain silent was overwhelming.

Sound familiar? We've all faced those moments when doing the right thing might cost us professionally. The good news? These ethical crossroads aren't just tests to endure—they're opportunities to demonstrate genuine leadership that builds trust and creates lasting value.

As we've explored throughout this book, Daniel navigated a complex ethical terrain while surviving and thriving in influence. His approach offers us valuable principles for our own ethical challenges. Let's consolidate these insights into a practical framework you can apply when facing tough choices.

INTRODUCING THE DANIEL FRAMEWORK

Based on the ethical principles we've seen throughout Daniel's story, this framework provides a structured approach to navigating complex moral challenges:

D - DEFINE THE ETHICAL ISSUE

Before rushing to solutions, get crystal clear about what's really at stake. Move beyond vague discomfort to precisely identify the principles or values being challenged.

When a pharmaceutical researcher discovered that clinical trial data for a new drug showed serious side effects being downplayed, they specifically defined the issue: "Presenting incomplete safety data violates scientific integrity and could potentially harm patients." This clarity gave them solid ground to stand on as they moved forward.

Key questions to ask:

- What specific ethical principles or values are being challenged?
- Who might be harmed if I make the wrong choice here?
- What precedent would this decision set for future situations?
- Am I facing a true ethical issue or simply a challenging business decision?

A - ANALYZE THE CONTEXT

Just as Daniel had to understand the political dynamics of

Babylon, you need to understand the full context surrounding your ethical challenge.

When a government procurement officer uncovered contracting irregularities in their department, they carefully analyzed the organizational culture, the history of similar situations, and the power dynamics at play. This contextual understanding helped them craft an approach that addressed the ethical concerns while working within the realities of their environment.

Key questions to ask:

- What cultural or organizational factors are influencing this situation?
- What historical context or precedents provide insight?
- What pressures or incentives might be driving others' perspectives?
- How might my own position or biases be shaping how I see this issue?

N - NAVIGATE COMPETING LOYALTIES

Most ethical challenges involve competing obligations. You might feel pulled between loyalty to your organization, colleagues, customers, professional standards, and personal values.

A sustainability officer at an energy company had to balance obligations to shareholders, colleagues, environmental responsibility, and their own integrity. By explicitly acknowledging these competing loyalties, you can prioritize them thoughtfully rather than being unconsciously swayed by the loudest or most immediate concerns.

Key questions to ask:

- What different loyalties am I experiencing in this situation?
- How would I rank these loyalties in terms of their ethical priority?
- Is there a way to honor multiple loyalties without compromising core principles?
- What loyalties might others in this situation be experiencing?

I - INVESTIGATE ALTERNATIVES

Ethical dilemmas often appear as binary choices: speak up or stay silent, proceed or withdraw, comply or resist. Daniel consistently found creative third options, like proposing a test period for his dietary preferences rather than simply accepting or rejecting the king's food.

When an emergency physician faced pressure to prioritize a politically connected patient over more critically injured victims during a crisis, they moved beyond the obvious binary choices. They created a solution that provided the VIP with excellent care while maintaining fair triage principles—a creative approach that upheld ethics while acknowledging practical realities.

Key questions to ask:

- What options exist beyond the obvious binary choices?
- What creative approaches might address both ethical concerns and practical needs?

- Who could I consult who might bring fresh perspective to this challenge?
- What would an ideal outcome look like, and how might we work toward it?

E - EVALUATE LONG-TERM CONSEQUENCES

While immediate outcomes matter, ethical leadership requires considering the extended impact of your choices. Daniel consistently looked beyond immediate risks to long-term implications.

When a technology director discovered concerning bias in their company's AI algorithm, they evaluated potential long-term consequences: harm to underrepresented groups, erosion of trust with customers, regulatory implications, and precedents for future ethical decisions. This broader evaluation helped them make a compelling case for addressing the issues thoroughly.

Key questions to ask:

- How might this decision affect stakeholder trust over time?
- What precedent would this decision establish for future situations?
- How might this choice affect organizational culture in the long run?
- What ripple effects might emerge from this decision?

L - LEAD WITH MORAL COURAGE

Knowledge without action—it isn't leadership. After working through the previous steps, ethical leadership requires the courage to act on your convictions, even when doing so carries personal or professional risk.

When a policy advisor discovered their senator's energy bill contained provisions that contradicted their public environmental commitments, they knew bringing this forward might damage their career. Despite these risks, they presented their concerns clearly, along with an alternative approach. This moral courage initially created tension but in the end strengthened both the legislation and their reputation as a trusted advisor.

Key questions to ask:

- What fears might be holding me back from taking ethical action?
- What support or resources do I need to follow through on my convictions?
- How can I communicate my position in a way that's both principled and respectful?
- How will I respond if my ethical stand meets with resistance or consequences?

APPLYING THE DANIEL FRAMEWORK: A STEP-BY-STEP GUIDE

Let's see how these principles might apply to a realistic scenario.

The Scenario

An operations director at a manufacturing company discovers that productivity targets are being met by quietly bypassing certain safety protocols. Their supervisor suggests this is just "finding efficiencies" and reminds them that bonuses depend on maintaining current production levels.

Step 1: Define the ethical issue

The operations director identifies several ethical principles at stake: employee safety, organizational integrity, honesty in reporting, and their professional responsibility as a leader.

Step 2: Analyze the context

The operations director considers several contextual factors:

- Industry history of similar compromises leading to accidents
- Company culture that emphasizes results over process
- Recent financial pressures after losing a major contract
- Their own responsibility for both safety outcomes and production targets

Step 3: Navigate Competing Loyalties

- The operations director acknowledges loyalties to:
- Their team's safety and wellbeing
- The company's financial success
- Their supervisor and leadership team
- Professional standards in operations management
- Their personal integrity and values around worker protection

Step 4: Investigate Alternatives

Rather than simply continuing the unsafe practices or reporting violations immediately, the operations director explores options:

- Conducting a safety-efficiency analysis to identify legitimate process improvements
- Developing a phased implementation of full safety compliance
- Consulting with safety experts on protocol modernization
- Creating transparent metrics that balance production and safety

Step 5: Evaluate long-term consequences

The operations director considers potential long-term impacts:

- Risk of workplace injuries or fatalities
- Legal and regulatory liability
- Employee trust and morale implications
- Precedent for how safety is valued in decision-making
- Personal ethical consequences of their choice

Step 6: Lead with moral courage

Based on this analysis, the operations director decides to:

1. Document the current safety compromises and their risks
2. Develop a proposal showing how proper safety protocols could be integrated with reasonable production targets
3. Present their findings and proposal to senior leadership
4. Make it clear they cannot continue overseeing operations that bypass critical safety measures

Though initially met with resistance, their thoughtful, solutions-oriented approach finally convinces leadership to reset production targets and invest in efficiency improvements that don't compromise safety. The company avoids potential disasters while developing safer processes that prove sustainable and legally compliant.

THE DANIEL FRAMEWORK AS A LEADERSHIP TOOL

The power of this framework isn't just in avoiding ethical mistakes—it's in changing challenges into opportunities for exceptional leadership.

When the operations director applied these principles, they didn't just prevent potential accidents; they helped their company develop new approaches to balancing safety and productivity. This pattern appears consistently when leaders apply the DANIEL Framework.

A researcher's stand on clinical trial data integrity led to discovering a more promising targeted application for the drug. A procurement officer's exposure of contracting irregularities created more transparent, cost-effective government processes. A sustainability director's environmental ethics stance positioned their company as an industry leader in responsible practices.

That's the potential of principled ethical leadership. It doesn't just prevent harm—it creates possibilities for growth, trust-building, and sustainable success that ethical compromise never could.

MAKING THE DANIEL FRAMEWORK YOUR OWN

This framework isn't a rigid formula but a flexible approach that becomes more natural with practice. Here are suggestions for integrating it into your leadership:

1. **Start with small decisions**. Apply these principles to everyday choices before facing major ethical crossroads.
2. **Create reflection space**. Ethical clarity often requires stepping back from immediate pressures. Build regular reflection time into your schedule.
3. **Find thinking partners**. Identify colleagues who share your commitment to ethical leadership. Regular conversations can sharpen your ethical reasoning.
4. **Study ethical exemplars**. Look for modern "Daniels" in your field who navigate complex challenges with integrity and wisdom.

Learn from experience. Keep notes on ethical challenges you face and how you navigate them to build your personal wisdom over time.

The journey of ethical leadership isn't always easy. There will be moments when doing the right thing feels costly or complicated. But as we've seen throughout this book, ethical leadership isn't just about avoiding wrong—it's about creating extraordinary possibilities for good.

By applying these principles consistently, you build more than just a better career. You create positive ripple effects that extend far beyond what you can currently see or imagine.

Are you ready to turn your next ethical challenge into an opportunity for exceptional leadership?

APPENDIX B: HISTORICAL CONTEXT OF DANIEL'S LIFE

STEPPING INTO DANIEL'S WORLD: A LEADERSHIP CONTEXT

I magine this scenario: You're suddenly relocated to a foreign country where you don't speak the language. Your new employer expects you to not only adapt quickly but excel in their corporate culture. Everything from the food in the cafeteria to the office rituals feels alien. Your core values clash with company practices, yet your career advancement depends on navigating this environment successfully.

Sound challenging? This was essentially Daniel's reality when he was taken from Jerusalem to Babylon around 605 BCE.

Understanding his historical context isn't just interesting background information. It's essential for appreciating the remarkable leadership skills he developed and how his strategies can reshape our approach to today's organizational challenges.

Let me invite you into Daniel's world and show you why his

ancient leadership journey feels surprisingly relevant to our modern professional landscapes.

THE ORGANIZATIONAL CULTURE OF BABYLON: POWER, POLITICS, AND PRESTIGE

When we talk about challenging workplace cultures today, they pale in comparison to what Daniel encountered in Babylon. The Neo-Babylonian Empire represented the ultimate hierarchical organization, with power concentrated at the top and swift consequences for those who failed to align with expectations.

Babylon itself was the ancient equivalent of a gleaming corporate headquarters designed to impress and intimidate. Its famous hanging gardens and massive ziggurat temples showcased engineering prowess that wouldn't be matched for centuries. The Ishtar Gate, with its brilliant blue glazed bricks and reliefs of lions and dragons, was designed to communicate power and divine authority to anyone entering the city.

For Daniel, arriving from the relatively modest city of Jerusalem, the cultural shock would be similar to someone from a small regional company suddenly joining a dominant global corporation with an entirely different culture and value system.

The Babylonian court where Daniel worked was the ultimate high-stakes environment:

- Leadership was absolute and often arbitrary.
- Political alliances shifted constantly.
- Success depended on both competence and carefully managed relationships.

- Consequences for missteps could be severe or even fatal.
- Ethical compromises were expected as part of "getting ahead."

What's fascinating is that Daniel didn't just survive in this environment. He thrived, rising to extraordinary influence while maintaining his integrity. His approach offers valuable insights for contemporary professionals navigating complex organizational cultures where their values often conflict with organizational expectations.

THE TALENT MANAGEMENT STRATEGY: BABYLON'S EXECUTIVE DEVELOPMENT PROGRAM

Daniel's presence in Babylon wasn't accidental. He was part of a sophisticated talent acquisition strategy that modern organizations would recognize immediately.

When Nebuchadnezzar conquered Jerusalem, he didn't just seize territory and resources. He implemented what we might today call a strategic talent acquisition plan. The Babylonian approach targeted high-potential individuals from conquered territories for a specialized development program.

The biblical text tells us they looked for "young men without physical defect, handsome, showing aptitude for every kind of learning, well-informed, quick to understand, and qualified to serve in the king's palace."

This "Babylonian Leadership Development Program" included:

- Language training in Aramaic and Babylonian.
- Immersion in local literature and cultural knowledge.

- Assigned Babylonian names to reinforce new identities.
- Premium food and accommodations to create loyalty.
- Intensive three-year curriculum before "graduation."

This wasn't just education. It was a comprehensive acculturation process designed to reshape promising foreigners into loyal Babylonian officials who would serve the empire's interests.

The parallels to modern corporate onboarding and development programs are striking. Many organizations today similarly try to reshape new talent to fit their culture, sometimes at the expense of individual identity and values.

Daniel's response to this pressure—it offers a masterclass in maintaining personal integrity while still delivering exceptional performance. When the program required eating food that violated his dietary principles, Daniel proposed an alternative that would allow him to maintain his values while still meeting performance expectations. This strategy of finding "third way" solutions would define his leadership approach throughout his career.

THE RELIGIOUS AND CULTURAL ENVIRONMENT: NAVIGATING COMPETING VALUE SYSTEMS

If the professional environment in Babylon was challenging, the cultural and religious landscape was even more complex for Daniel. Babylon was thoroughly polytheistic, with gods and goddesses governing every aspect of life. Religious observances weren't private matters but central to public life and political identity.

For Daniel, raised in the monotheistic tradition of Israel, this created constant ethical tension. Consider what he faced:

His Babylonian name, Belteshazzar, honored a pagan deity.

- Court rituals often included religious elements he couldn't in good conscience participate in.
- Career advancement typically required religious conformity.
- His dietary restrictions marked him as different in a culture that valued assimilation.
- His prayer practices could be (and eventually were) portrayed as political disloyalty.

Many professionals today face similar challenges when organizational values conflict with personal convictions. Like the employee whose company culture glorifies metrics at the expense of customer care, or the manager asked to implement policies that undermine team wellbeing in service of short-term profits, Daniel constantly navigated tension between competing value systems.

What makes Daniel's approach remarkable is that he didn't choose either total assimilation or rigid opposition. Instead, he discerned which cultural adaptations were acceptable and which crossed his ethical boundaries. He became culturally fluent without compromising core principles.

Today's leaders can learn from this balanced approach when navigating organizations where some practices align with their values while others create ethical tension.

THE POLITICAL DYNAMICS: LEADERSHIP THROUGH REGIME CHANGE

One of the most instructive aspects of Daniel's career was his ability to maintain influence through dramatic leadership transitions. His career spanned the reigns of at least four kings and a major regime change when the Persian Empire conquered Babylon in 539 BCE.

Think about how challenging organizational mergers and CEO transitions can be in modern contexts. Now multiply that challenge several times over and you'll appreciate what Daniel accomplished by remaining influential across multiple administrations.

The Babylonian administrative structure under Nebuchadnezzar included:

- The king with ultimate authority.
- A royal council of advisors with specialized expertise.
- Regional governors overseeing territories.
- Local officials handling day-to-day administration.

Daniel rose through these ranks to become a trusted royal advisor, known for both his technical expertise (interpreting dreams and visions) and his administrative capabilities.

When the Persians conquered Babylon under Cyrus the Great, they implemented significant organizational restructuring. The new Persian system established more standardized provinces (satrapies) with appointed governors (satraps). Under Darius, Daniel was appointed as one of three administrators supervising 120 satraps, essentially becoming one of the top executives in the largest empire the world had yet seen.

This remarkable ability to maintain and even increase influence through regime changes offers valuable lessons for modern professionals navigating mergers, acquisitions, and leadership transitions. Daniel's reputation for integrity, competence, and wisdom transcended political allegiances, making him valuable to successive administrations despite his foreign origin.

CULTURAL INTELLIGENCE: HONOR, SHAME, AND LEADERSHIP CAPITAL

To fully appreciate Daniel's leadership accomplishments, we need to understand the honor-shame cultural system he navigated. Unlike our relatively individualistic modern contexts, Daniel operated in a collectivist society where:

- Personal identity derived primarily from group membership.
- Public perception and reputation were paramount.
- Loyalty to patrons and superiors was a core virtue.
- Saving face (avoiding shame) drove many decisions.
- Reciprocal obligations created elaborate social networks.

When Daniel refused the king's food or declined to stop praying despite the royal decree, he wasn't just making personal religious choices. He was navigating complex cultural expectations where refusing royal benefaction could be seen as rejecting the social relationship itself—a serious breach of cultural norms.

Daniel's ability to decline royal provisions while maintaining respect for authority, or to disobey a decree while demonstrating loyalty to the king himself, shows remarkable cultural intelligence. He found ways to maintain his core principles while honoring the underlying cultural values of respect and proper relationship.

Leaders working in multicultural environments can learn from Daniel's approach. He understood the cultural system deeply enough to work within it effectively while still maintaining his non-negotiable values.

THE ETHICAL LANDSCAPE: ECONOMIC JUSTICE AND POWER DYNAMICS

The Babylonian and Persian Empires, like all ancient super-powers, were built on economic extraction from conquered territories. The wealth displayed in the imperial capitals came largely from tribute, taxation, and control of trade routes.

As an administrator whose responsibilities likely included economic oversight, Daniel faced ethical challenges related to systemic inequality. How could he serve effectively within imperial systems while maintaining the Hebrew ethical tradition's emphasis on justice and care for the vulnerable?

The text doesn't directly address how Daniel handled specific economic policies, but his reputation for incorruptibility suggests he found ways to administer justly within imperfect systems. This parallels the challenges many leaders face when working within organizational structures that have problematic aspects while trying to influence them toward greater equity and justice.

DANIEL'S LEADERSHIP MASTERCLASS: FINDING PURPOSE IN THE PRESSURE COOKER

What makes Daniel's story so compelling for modern ethical leadership is his status as someone who had to navigate between competing worlds and value systems:

- He was ethnically Jewish but serving in Babylonian and Persian administrations.
- He maintained monotheistic faith while functioning in polytheistic systems.
- He exercised political authority while coming from a conquered people.
- He preserved cultural distinctiveness while adapting to foreign contexts.

This "between worlds" status creates the ethical tension that runs throughout his story. Daniel wasn't making leadership decisions from a position of perfect freedom or autonomy. He operated within significant constraints, facing pressures and consequences that could have been career-ending or even life-threatening.

His leadership wasn't theoretical; it was practical wisdom applied in real-world power dynamics where the stakes were extraordinarily high. He didn't have the luxury of abstract moral reasoning divorced from consequences. Every ethical stand potentially carried life-altering implications.

That's why Daniel's example speaks so powerfully to today's leaders. Most of us make ethical decisions within organizational constraints, not in conditions of perfect freedom. We navigate competing loyalties, imperfect systems, and situations where both action and inaction carry consequences.

WHY DANIEL'S CONTEXT MATTERS FOR MODERN LEADERS

Understanding the historical context of Daniel's leadership journey offers several key insights for navigating today's complex organizational landscapes:

1. **Cultural intelligence determines effectiveness.** Daniel's success came partly from his ability to understand Babylonian culture deeply enough to know where he could adapt and where he needed to draw ethical lines. Similarly, today's leaders need to understand their organizational cultures to navigate them effectively.

2. **Systems shape ethical choices.** Many of Daniel's ethical dilemmas emerged from the systems and structures he inhabited. Understanding your organizational systems and how they create ethical pressure points is essential for navigating them effectively.

3. **Power dynamics are always present.** Daniel navigated complex power relationships where various stakeholders had different agendas. Ethical leadership requires recognizing these dynamics rather than pretending they don't exist.

4. **Identity anchors ethics.** Daniel's clear sense of identity as a servant of God provided his ethical anchor. What core identities and values anchor your leadership decisions when organizational pressures push toward compromise?

5. **Constraints foster creativity.** Daniel often found creative "third ways" when faced with seemingly binary choices between compliance and defiance. The

constraints he faced fostered ethical creativity rather than limiting it.

APPLYING DANIEL'S HISTORICAL CONTEXT TODAY

When you face ethical challenges in your organization, remember that you're not the first leader to navigate complex moral terrain within powerful systems. Daniel's example shows that it's possible to maintain integrity while serving effectively, even in environments that sometimes conflict with your deepest values.

The historical context doesn't diminish Daniel's ethical leadership. It makes it all the more remarkable and relevant. By understanding the world he navigated, we gain deeper appreciation for the wisdom, courage, and discernment his choices required. And we find more applicable strategies for our own leadership challenges today.

Next time you're facing an ethical dilemma at work, wondering how to balance organizational expectations with your core values, remember Daniel. His journey from captive to cabinet secretary, maintaining integrity through regime changes and life-threatening challenges, offers a blueprint for leadership that changes constraints into opportunities and converts ethical stands into expanded influence.

APPENDIX C: CONTEMPORARY CASE STUDIES IN ETHICAL LEADERSHIP

INTRODUCTION: ANCIENT WISDOM FOR MODERN CHALLENGES

I remember sitting with a senior executive after she had navigated a particularly thorny ethical dilemma. Over coffee, she confided, "I wish someone had handed me a roadmap for this journey years ago. I've had to piece together wisdom from so many sources along the way."

Her words stayed with me because they capture what this collection of case studies aims to provide: a practical roadmap for your ethical leadership journey.

Each story represents real situations (with names and identifying details changed) where leaders faced consequential ethical decisions that tested their core values. What makes these stories particularly valuable is how they illustrate Daniel's ancient principles in action across diverse modern contexts. They show that integrity isn't just morally right but often strategically advantageous in ways that compromise never achieves.

As you read these studies, you might recognize situations similar to challenges you've faced or may encounter. My hope is that they offer not just inspiration but practical strategies for navigating your own ethical crossroads with both principle and wisdom.

CASE STUDY 1: THE PHARMACEUTICAL WHISTLEBLOWER

Presented as journal entries to reveal inner ethical struggle

FROM THE JOURNAL OF DR. ROBERT LIANG, SENIOR RESEARCH SCIENTIST

March 15

The preliminary analysis of Neurozen's Phase III data crossed my desk today. Something doesn't look right. The neurological side effect patterns that concerned me in earlier trials seem to be continuing, but they're buried in the statistical noise. Most people wouldn't notice, but after fifteen years in clinical research, certain patterns jump out at me. I've flagged it for Eleanor to review tomorrow.

March 17

Met with Eleanor this morning. Her response was concerning. "These findings are statistically insignificant, Robert. We've invested hundreds of millions in Neurozen. The company's future depends on this approval."

There was something in her tone that felt dismissive, almost warning me away from this line of inquiry. I need to look deeper before raising this again.

March 22

I can barely sleep. After comparing the raw data with the processed reports, I've found clear evidence that someone altered the original findings to minimize the appearance of side effects.

When I confronted Eleanor, she actually admitted knowing about the changes but defended them as "data cleaning." Then she reminded me about my bonus and future prospects at Helix. The subtext was clear: stay quiet or pay the price.

I keep thinking about my father, who suffered from similar neurological symptoms for years. What if his doctors had prescribed a medication with known risks that had been deliberately concealed? The thought makes me physically ill.

Tonight I read about Daniel refusing the king's food, his first ethical stand in Babylon. What strikes me is how he created an alternative rather than just saying no. I need to find a constructive path forward, not just oppose what's happening.

March 24

I've spent two days developing a thorough alternative approach: disclose the side effects, request more targeted trials to identify which patient populations might be at risk, and potentially reposition Neurozen for specific conditions where benefits clearly outweigh risks.

This approach could actually create a more sustainable path to approval while protecting patients. Tomorrow I present this to senior leadership.

I'm rehearsing how to frame this as an opportunity rather than just a problem. I need to acknowledge legitimate business concerns while holding firm on scientific integrity. Much like Daniel with the Babylonian officials, I want to be respectful yet unwavering.

April 2

My presentation to senior leadership went nowhere. They dismissed my concerns and alternative approach. I've documented everything and submitted my findings to both the FDA and our ethics hotline.

I'm now on "administrative leave" pending an investigation. Colleagues are avoiding me. My career at Helix appears to be over.

Did I make the right choice? Daniel had divine intervention in the lions' den. I have no such guarantee. But I keep coming back to a simple truth: if we knowingly conceal safety risks, patients will be harmed. Some ethical boundaries simply can't be crossed, regardless of the consequences.

January 15, One Year Later

I received a job offer today from Intuitive Biotech, a startup committed to ethical drug development. Their CEO actually cited my whistleblowing case as one reason they wanted me: "We need scientists who prioritize integrity over expediency."

The FDA investigation led to a complete overhaul at Helix. The new leadership implemented rigorous data integrity protocols, and several executives resigned. Neurozen eventually received approval for targeted applications where its benefits clearly outweigh risks.

Looking back, what seemed like career suicide became the foundation for something better. I couldn't have predicted this outcome, but I've learned something profound: ethical leadership isn't about calculating personal advantage but about honoring deeper commitments, even when doing so carries significant risk.

BUILDING ETHICAL MUSCLE: LEADERSHIP LESSONS THROUGH METAPHOR

Think of ethical boundaries like the structural supports in a building. Dr. Liang discovered what Daniel knew centuries earlier: some load-bearing walls simply cannot be removed without compromising the entire structure. Scientific integrity wasn't just one value among many but a foundation that supported everything else.

Ethical leadership also requires the architectural skill of creative design. When existing plans prove problematic, leaders like Robert and Daniel don't simply criticize but develop alternative blueprints that address legitimate concerns while maintaining core principles.

Building ethical structures also requires proper documentation. Robert's meticulous record-keeping proved essential when investigations began, much as Daniel's consistent pattern of integrity created a record that spoke for itself when his enemies sought to undermine him.

Finally, ethical buildings often face severe testing. Robert weathered the storm of professional isolation and career uncertainty. What looked like structural failure initially proved to be a stronger foundation for his future career and for industry-wide integrity reforms.

The question isn't whether your ethical leadership will face testing, but whether you've developed the structural integrity to withstand those inevitable storms.

CASE STUDY 2: THE SUPPLY CHAIN ETHICS DILEMMA

Presented as a retrospective interview five years after the events

"FINDING THE THIRD PATH": AN INTERVIEW WITH PAMELA WILLIAMS, FORMER VP OF GLOBAL SUPPLY CHAIN

Interviewer: Thanks for joining us today, Pamela. Five years ago, your audit of Meridian Apparel's manufacturing partners uncovered serious ethical issues throughout your supply chain. What was going through your mind when you first realized the scope of the problem?

Pamela: It felt like opening Pandora's box, honestly. What started as a standard review after a competitor's factory disaster quickly revealed unsafe working conditions, wage violations, excessive overtime, and environmental compliance issues across multiple facilities. These weren't isolated incidents but systemic problems.

The most challenging part was knowing that addressing these issues would cost $30-45 million over three years. In fast fashion, where margins are already tight, that's a substantial hit. I remember our CFO arguing that implementing such changes would reduce margins by 3-4%, potentially threatening our competitive position.

Interviewer: So you faced significant resistance to making changes?

Pamela: Absolutely. The CEO proposed what many companies do: a PR-friendly sustainability initiative centered on a few showcase factories while gradually implementing changes elsewhere over a much longer timeframe. It would have generated positive press while minimizing short-term financial impact.

I knew this approach would leave thousands of workers in potentially dangerous conditions. But pushing too hard risked being sidelined or replaced by someone less committed to reform.

Interviewer: That sounds like a classic ethical dilemma with no good options. How did you approach it?

Pamela: I realized I was falling into the trap of seeing only two options: accept window dressing or push for immediate thorough reform and probably get fired. Daniel's approach in the biblical story offered a different perspective.

Instead of accepting this false binary, I started building coalitions around shared values. I met individually with our Chief Marketing Officer and Chief Human Resources Officer, framing ethical supply chain management as essential to brand integrity and talent retention. Both already had concerns about our practices but hadn't found an effective way to address them.

I also gathered compelling evidence showing how supply chain scandals had impacted competitor valuations and market share. Most importantly, I collected data on changing consumer preferences, particularly among younger demographics who increasingly prioritize ethical production.

Interviewer: So you changed it from an ethical issue into a business issue?

Pamela: Not exactly. It was always both. I refused to separate ethics from business because they're fundamentally connected. What I did was demonstrate how our ethical and business interests aligned rather than conflicted.

Instead of accepting the binary choice between thorough reform or window dressing, I developed a phased implementation plan that prioritized critical safety issues immediately while addressing other concerns through a transparent three-year roadmap.

Interviewer: How did leadership respond?

Pamela: After several tense weeks of negotiations, the executive committee approved a modified version of my plan: immediate remediation of critical safety issues, transparent public commitments with specific benchmarks, quarterly progress reporting to the board, a modest price increase on premium items to help offset costs, and collaboration with industry partners to share compliance costs.

Implementation wasn't easy. Two suppliers terminated their relationship with us rather than meet the new standards. We missed earnings projections for two consecutive quarters as we absorbed implementation costs.

Interviewer: That must have created substantial pressure to backtrack.

Pamela: It did. There were definitely moments when I questioned whether we'd made the right choice. But the longer-term impacts proved remarkably positive.

Our transparent approach earned praise from industry watchdogs and favorable media coverage. Internal surveys showed significantly higher company pride and reduced turnover, particularly among younger employees.

Factories that embraced the changes reported higher productivity and quality, partially offsetting the increased costs. When new legislation required supply chain due diligence, we were already compliant while competitors scrambled to catch up.

After initial margin pressure, our market position strengthened. Three years after implementing the changes, our stock had outperformed the industry average by 22%.

Interviewer: Looking back five years later, what key insights would you share with leaders facing similar ethical challenges?

Pamela: First, ethical leadership requires strategic patience. Change rarely happens overnight, but steady, principled pressure can change systems over time.

Second, evidence matters tremendously. My data-driven approach made ethical concerns harder to dismiss as merely idealistic.

Third, external forces can become powerful allies. Regulatory trends, consumer preferences, and industry standards helped strengthen my case for change.

Fourth, compromise on timing but not on principles. I accepted a longer implementation timeline but maintained my commitment to substantive change.

Finally, ethical leadership creates unexpected alliances. People who might disagree on other issues often rally around leaders with clear moral conviction.

Interviewer: Any final thoughts for leaders navigating their own ethical challenges?

Pamela: Remember that ethical leadership isn't about being perfect or having all the answers. It's about maintaining clear principles while finding practical paths forward.

Daniel didn't expect supernatural intervention when he refused to compromise. He simply did what was right and discovered that integrity created possibilities that compromise never could. I've found the same to be true in the corporate world. Ethical leadership isn't just right, it's in the end more successful.

CASE STUDY 3: THE TECH COMPANY'S PRIVACY CROSSROADS

Presented as a leadership team discussion

PRIVACY VS. PROFIT: A LEADERSHIP TEAM DIALOGUE

The following is a reconstructed dialogue from a critical meeting at Keystone Digital, a technology company whose marketing analytics platform faced an ethical crisis when leadership proposed monetizing user data in ways that violated the spirit of their privacy promises.

CEO: "Let's get straight to the point. Our growth has plateaued, and the board is pushing for new revenue streams. The proposal to combine user data with information from data brokers would allow us to create thorough profiles that advertisers would pay premium rates for. Legal confirms we can implement this by updating our terms of service. Users would automatically agree unless they opt out within 30 days."

Chief Revenue Officer: "Every company in our space does this. We're actually behind the curve. Users don't really care about privacy anyway. They just click 'agree' without reading."

Neville Johnson (Chief Privacy Officer): "I'd like to challenge that assumption. Our entire value proposition has been built on respecting user privacy. We explicitly promised users control over their personal information. This change may comply with the letter of our terms but violates their spirit entirely."

Chief Marketing Officer: "Neville has a point about our brand promise. Our marketing has emphasized privacy as a key differentiator. This pivot could undermine trust we've spent years building."

Chief Revenue Officer: "Trust doesn't pay the bills. Our competitors are monetizing data much more aggressively and growing faster. We need to evolve or get left behind."

Neville: "I understand the business pressures, but consider this through Daniel's framework. When he interpreted dreams for Babylonian kings, he provided insight without manipulation. He respected their agency even when he disagreed with their choices. What we're proposing here fundamentally disrespects our users' agency by assuming their consent through deliberately obscure terms updates."

General Counsel: "That's a philosophical position, Neville. Legally, we're covered as long as we provide notification and an opt-out mechanism."

Neville: "Legal compliance is necessary but not sufficient for ethical leadership. Daniel maintained clear ethical boundaries while finding creative ways to serve within Babylonian systems. We can do the same."

CEO: "What exactly are you proposing, Neville?"

Neville: "Instead of automatic opt-in to expanded data sharing, let's create genuine value exchanges. Offer transparent choices: improved services for those who choose to share more data, and continued basic services for those who don't.

"We could develop privacy-friendly analytics techniques that deliver advertiser value without thorough profiles. And we should be crystal clear about what data we collect and how we use it, in plain language rather than legal jargon."

Chief Technology Officer: "Those privacy-preserving analytics approaches might actually solve some technical challenges we've been facing with traditional methods. There's interesting research showing differential privacy techniques that could differentiate us in the market."

Chief Revenue Officer: "But will it generate enough revenue? That's the bottom line."

Neville: "There's growing evidence that privacy-focused business models build more sustainable value. Companies that respect user agency are seeing improved customer loyalty, reduced regulatory risk, and stronger brand equity. Short-term revenue gains from aggressive data monetization often lead to user backlash, regulatory penalties, and long-term brand damage."

CEO: "You've made compelling points, but we need immediate revenue growth. We're proceeding with the policy change but will incorporate some of your suggested modifications to reduce the most obvious risks. Users will receive notification of updated terms."

Three months after the meeting, a technology journal published an exposé on data practices in the industry, specifically highlighting Keystone Digital's policy change as a case study in "privacy bait-and-switch." The article sparked investigations by regulatory agencies and a sharp decline in Keystone Digital's stock price.

The board called an emergency meeting and asked Neville to present a path forward. Drawing on his earlier recommendations, he outlined a complete privacy reset that included:

- Reverting to a more transparent data policy
- Giving users genuine control over their information
- Offering clear value in exchange for data sharing
- Establishing an external ethics advisory board
- Positioning privacy protection as a competitive advantage

After significant internal debate, the company adopted Neville's approach.

The implementation was painful. Keystone Digital had to rebuild trust with users and weather continued regulatory scrutiny. Revenue projections were revised downward for the next two quarters.

FOUR DECISION PATHWAYS: QUESTIONS FOR ETHICAL NAVIGATION

When facing similar ethical crossroads in your organization, consider these four decision pathways that emerge from both Neville's experience and Daniel's ancient example:

Path 1: Values Clarity

- What core values define your organization's relationship with stakeholders?
- Which of these values are truly non-negotiable rather than merely preferred?
- How might short-term pressures be subtly eroding these foundational values?

- What would maintaining these values look like in this specific situation?

Path 2: Stakeholder Impact

- Whose trust might be damaged by expedient decisions?
- What information asymmetries exist between your organization and those it serves?
- How would you feel if you were on the receiving end of this decision?
- What long-term relationship damage might result from short-term gain?

Path 3: Creative Alternatives

- What "both/and" solutions might exist beyond the apparent "either/or" options?
- How might ethical boundaries actually inspire creativity rather than restrict it?
- What models exist in other contexts for addressing similar tensions?
- Who else should be involved in developing alternatives to conventional approaches?

Path 4: Courage and Communication

- How can you frame ethical concerns in language that resonates with decision-makers?
- What evidence would make your case more compelling to those with different priorities?
- How might you remain both respectful and firm when presenting ethical concerns?

- What documentation should you maintain regarding your position and recommendations?

Neville's experience at Keystone Digital illustrates what eventually happened at the company: The initial painful transition to a more ethical approach led to industry leadership, regulatory influence, product innovation, and talent advantages that created sustainable growth.

While initial growth was slower than competitors taking more aggressive approaches, Keystone Digital established a more sustainable business model less vulnerable to regulatory shifts and consumer backlash.

Like Daniel, whose consistent ethical position proved valuable during political transitions, Neville's ethical expertise became more rather than less valuable after the company faced a crisis.

CASE STUDY 4: THE GOVERNMENT CONTRACTOR'S INTEGRITY TEST

Presented in traditional narrative format with ethical principles embedded in the story

THE ALGORITHM'S MORAL CODE

Elijah Washington stood at his office window, watching the fading light reflect off the mirrored buildings of the business park. As Project Director at Guardian Integrated Solutions, a defense contractor developing surveillance systems for government agencies, he had just discovered something deeply troubling about their flagship project, a facial recognition platform for border security.

During system testing, his team uncovered significant algorithmic bias, with dramatically higher error rates for certain demographic groups. These errors could lead to serious consequences, including wrongful detentions and privacy violations disproportionately affecting specific communities.

When Elijah brought these findings to his superiors, he received a concerning response: "The contract doesn't specify accuracy requirements by demographic. We're exceeding the overall accuracy benchmarks, and that's what matters. Delaying delivery to fix these issues would trigger penalty clauses and possibly jeopardize the entire contract."

The company's leadership argued that the government agency could determine acceptable risk levels, and Guardian's job was simply to deliver what was contractually required. They proposed noting the limitations in technical documentation while proceeding with deployment.

Elijah recognized this approach might satisfy contractual requirements but would potentially result in discriminatory impacts. However, challenging a major government contract could threaten hundreds of jobs and the company's future viability.

As an African American man who had experienced algorithmic bias firsthand, Elijah felt a personal connection to the issue. Before joining Guardian, he had been incorrectly flagged by a security system at a technical conference, a humiliating experience that highlighted how these seemingly abstract technical issues created real human impacts.

The principles that had guided Daniel in ancient Babylon now illuminated Elijah's path through this modern ethical maze:

Technical excellence creates ethical capital. Like Daniel, whose extraordinary capability gave him a platform for influence, Elijah's technical expertise and successful project management record gave him credibility when raising ethical concerns. He wasn't seen as an idealist disconnected from business realities but as a respected technical leader whose concerns warranted attention.

With this foundation, Elijah prepared a thorough analysis documenting the algorithmic bias issues, their potential real-world impacts, and the technical approaches needed to address them. Rather than presenting this as an ethical critique, he framed it as a previously unidentified technical risk that could affect contract performance and create liability for both Guardian and the government agency.

Framing matters tremendously in ethical influence. Daniel presented his refusal to eat the king's food not as religious stubbornness but as an opportunity to demonstrate better health outcomes. Similarly, Elijah presented ethical concerns as business and technical risks, making them harder to dismiss as merely personal values. This approach respected legitimate business priorities while maintaining his ethical boundaries.

Elijah requested a meeting with the company's CEO and General Counsel. When they remained resistant, he took a calculated risk: "I understand the contractual and financial pressures. However, I believe we have a legal and ethical obligation to disclose these issues to the client. If we don't, I will not certify the system as project director, which will create contractual problems regardless."

Strategic leverage can serve ethical ends. Daniel's unwavering commitment to his principles created leverage precisely because everyone knew he wouldn't compromise. Elijah's willingness to withhold his technical certification created necessary leverage for ethical considerations that might otherwise have been ignored in the rush to complete the contract.

This created a difficult impasse. Replacing Elijah would cause significant project disruption, but accepting his position meant potential contract complications. After tense deliberations, the executive team agreed to a modified approach:

- Disclose the demographic accuracy issues to the government client
- Propose a phased deployment with higher human oversight in areas where algorithmic bias had been identified
- Establish a parallel workstream to improve algorithmic performance across demographics
- Create an ethics advisory panel to review future projects for similar issues

Ethical leadership includes practical compromise. Like Daniel finding workable solutions within Babylonian court life, Elijah developed an approach that addressed core ethical concerns while acknowledging business realities. He understood that perfect solutions rarely exist in complex organizations, but integrity doesn't require absolute purity, just clear boundaries around non-negotiable values.

The government client's initial reaction was frustration over potential delays. However, after considering the political and legal risks of deploying a system with documented bias, they agreed to the modified approach with adjusted timelines.

Process changes outlast individual decisions. The most significant outcome wasn't just addressing this specific algorithm's bias but creating institutional changes that would affect future projects. Guardian Integrated Solutions established more robust ethical review processes and eventually created a Chief Ethics Officer position with Elijah's input.

The longer-term outcomes were mixed but in the end positive. Though modified in scope and timeline, the core contract remained intact, protecting jobs and company stability. The focused effort to address algorithmic bias led to new approaches that improved the system's overall performance. The case became a reference point in developing standards for algorithmic impact assessments in government contracts.

While initially facing internal resistance, Elijah eventually received a promotion and became known in the industry as a leader who could balance technical excellence with ethical considerations, much as Daniel's principled approach eventually led to greater rather than diminished influence.

The case reminds us that ethical dilemmas rarely present themselves as obvious choices between pure good and evident evil. More often, they emerge as tensions between competing values, each with legitimate claims. In those situations, leaders like Elijah and Daniel demonstrate that principled navigation requires both moral clarity about essential boundaries and practical wisdom about implementation.

Most importantly, both stories illustrate that ethical leadership isn't about maintaining personal purity at the expense of practical impact. It's about leveraging clear principles into constructive solutions that change systems rather than merely critiquing them from a distance.

CONCLUSION: THE RIPPLE EFFECTS OF ETHICAL LEADERSHIP

As we've seen through these diverse case studies, ethical leadership creates ripple effects that extend far beyond individual decisions or careers. Whether through Robert's journaling process, Pamela's strategic patience, Neville's principled stand, or Elijah's technical approach, each leader discovered what Daniel knew centuries ago: integrity isn't just morally right but pragmatically powerful.

Several common themes emerge across these different contexts:

First, ethical leadership often begins with individual conviction but extends to systemic impact. What started as one person's ethical stand led to organizational and sometimes industry-wide changes that benefited many others.

Second, ethical leadership requires both courage and wisdom. Effective ethical leaders don't just take principled stands; they navigate complex situations with strategic thinking and careful implementation.

Third, constructive approaches amplify ethical influence. Those who propose solutions rather than simply identifying problems have greater impact and face less isolation.

Finally, ethical capital accumulates over time. Leaders who maintain consistent ethical positions gain increasing influence even when specific stands are initially rejected.

As you face your own ethical challenges, remember these modern "Daniels" who navigated complex organizational pressures while maintaining their integrity. Their experiences confirm that principled leadership isn't just morally right, it's often the most successful approach for creating sustainable success in our complex, interconnected world.

The choice to lead with integrity, wisdom, and courage may not always be easy, but as these case studies demonstrate, it creates possibilities for positive impact that ethical compromise never could.

Like Daniel in ancient Babylon, you have the opportunity to change ethical challenges into leadership opportunities that ripple far beyond your immediate circumstances.

APPENDIX D: RESOURCES FOR ETHICAL LEADERSHIP

Every ethical leader needs practical resources to support their development journey. In my years of mentoring executives through challenging moral terrain, I've observed that the most successful leaders aren't necessarily those with the clearest initial answers, but those who know how to access wisdom and guidance when facing complexity. They build personal libraries of reliable resources they can turn to when confronting unfamiliar ethical challenges.

This carefully curated collection represents the most valuable tools, frameworks, and references I've discovered for developing ethical leadership capabilities. Rather than an exhaustive academic bibliography, I've selected resources based on their practical value, accessibility, and relevance to the principles explored throughout this book.

Think of this as your personal ethical leadership library, organized by key areas of development. Each recommendation includes a brief explanation of why it's valuable and how you can access it today.

UNDERSTANDING ETHICAL FRAMEWORKS

These resources help you build a strong foundation in ethical reasoning, giving you the conceptual tools to navigate complex moral terrain.

BOOKS YOU'LL ACTUALLY ENJOY READING

"Justice: What's the Right Thing to Do?" by Michael Sandel (2010)

Imagine discussing life's toughest ethical questions with a brilliant friend who never makes you feel inadequate. That's the experience of reading Sandel's accessible exploration of different ethical frameworks. Like Daniel navigating between Jewish and Babylonian worldviews, this book helps you understand how different traditions approach moral questions.

Available from most booksellers and libraries.

"How Good People Make Tough Choices" by Rushworth M. Kidder (2009)

When you're facing those "right vs. right" dilemmas where two valid principles conflict, this book is like having a wise mentor at your side. Kidder provides frameworks that would have served Daniel well as he balanced competing obligations to earthly authorities and divine commands.

Available in print, e-book, and audiobook formats.

"The Power of Ethics: How to Make Good Choices in a Complicated World" by Susan Liautaud (2021)

This newer addition to the ethics library delivers practical guidance for navigating today's complex ethical landscape.

Liautaud combines compelling stories with clear frameworks that help you apply ethical thinking to modern challenges.

Available from most booksellers.

ONLINE RESOURCES YOU CAN ACCESS TODAY

Stanford Encyclopedia of Philosophy: Ethics Section

plato.stanford.edu/entries/ethics

This free, authoritative resource offers in-depth yet accessible explorations of ethical concepts. The entries on virtue ethics, deontology, consequentialism, and professional ethics provide excellent foundations for anyone seeking to deepen their understanding.

The Ethics Centre

ethics.org.au

This Australian nonprofit offers free resources including decision-making frameworks, case studies, and articles on contemporary ethical issues. Their "Ethics Explainer" series is particularly helpful for quickly grasping key concepts.

Markkula Center for Applied Ethics

scu.edu/ethics

Santa Clara University's ethics center offers frameworks, articles, and case studies across various domains including business, technology, healthcare, and government. Their "Ethics App" provides a step-by-step approach to ethical decision-making.

ETHICAL DECISION-MAKING

These resources offer practical frameworks and approaches for making sound ethical decisions in complex situations.

BOOKS THAT IMPROVE DECISION-MAKING

"Giving Voice to Values" by Mary C. Gentile (2010)

Rather than focusing only on identifying the right thing to do, Gentile helps you develop skills for effectively acting on your values. The book includes practical exercises that would have resonated with Daniel's ability to maintain principles while working within existing power structures.

Available in print and digital formats.

"Thinking in Bets" by Annie Duke (2018)

While not explicitly about ethics, this book revolutionizes decision-making under uncertainty. Duke's insights about recognizing our cognitive biases and making decisions with incomplete information apply beautifully to ethical dilemmas.

Available in print, e-book, and audiobook formats.

"Ethical Intelligence" by Bruce Weinstein (2011)

Weinstein provides a framework based on five principles of ethical intelligence, with practical applications across various professional contexts. The straightforward approach makes complex ethical reasoning accessible.

Available from most booksellers.

ONLINE COURSES YOU CAN START TODAY

"Ethical Leadership: Character, Civility, and Community" (University of Virginia on Coursera)

coursera.org/learn/ethical-leadership

This course examines how leaders can develop and strengthen the ethical aspects of their leadership. You can audit the course for free or pay for a certificate of completion.

"Ethical Decision-Making for Global Managers" (University of Illinois on Coursera)

coursera.org/learn/ethical-decision-making-global-managers

This course helps leaders navigate ethical challenges in global contexts, particularly valuable for those working in multicultural environments as Daniel did. Free to audit, with optional paid certificate.

"Ethics in the Workplace" (LinkedIn Learning)

linkedin.com/learning/ethics-in-the-workplace

This concise course offers practical guidance for everyday ethical challenges. Available with LinkedIn Learning subscription, which often comes free with LinkedIn Premium or through many public libraries.

PRACTICAL TOOLS AND FRAMEWORKS

The Markkula Center for Applied Ethics Decision Framework

scu.edu/ethics/ethics-resources/ethical-decision-making

This practical, free framework walks through key considerations for ethical decision-making, including recognizing ethical issues, evaluating alternative actions, and reflecting on outcomes.

Ethical OS Toolkit

ethicalos.org

Now maintained by the Institute for the Future, this toolkit helps teams anticipate potential ethical issues, particularly in technology development. The latest version is available for free download on their website.

Ethics Unwrapped - Ethics Defined Video Series

ethicsunwrapped.utexas.edu/ethics-defined

Short, engaging videos explaining key ethical concepts and frameworks. Perfect for quick learning or sharing with teams. All videos are freely available online.

BUILDING ETHICAL ORGANIZATIONAL CULTURES

These resources focus on how leaders can foster ethical cultures within their organizations.

BOOKS THAT SHAPE ORGANIZATIONS

"The Business of Ethics" by Judith White and Susan Summers (2016)

This practical guide helps leaders understand how ethical cultures contribute to organizational success. Like Daniel's influence on the empires he served, it provides approaches for developing integrity-based cultures.

Available in print and e-book formats.

"Blind Spots: Why We Fail to Do What's Right and What to Do about It" by Max H. Bazerman and Ann E. Tenbrunsel (2011)

This book explores psychological factors that lead to ethical failures and provides strategies for addressing systematic biases.

Available from most booksellers.

"The Power of Ethics Culture" by Bernard Boisson (2022)

This newer work explores how organizational culture shapes ethical behavior and provides a roadmap for building cultures where integrity thrives.

Available in print and digital formats.

ORGANIZATIONS AND NETWORKS

Business Ethics Network (BEN)

businessethicsnetwork.org

This global network connects ethics and compliance professionals, providing resources, best practices, and networking opportunities. Free resources are available on their website, with additional benefits for members.

Ethics & Compliance Initiative (ECI)

ethics.org

ECI offers research, resources, and certification programs focused on building ethical cultures in organizations. Their Ethics Resource Center provides free access to research reports and best practices.

Conscious Capitalism

consciouscapitalism.org

This organization promotes business practices that elevate humanity through higher ethical standards. Their website offers free resources, and local chapters provide networking opportunities.

SPEAKING TRUTH TO POWER

These resources provide guidance for effectively raising ethical concerns with those in positions of authority.

BOOKS THAT BUILD COURAGE

"Courageous Conversations" by Sarah Noll Wilson (2022)

This recent publication provides frameworks for having difficult conversations about important issues. Wilson combines psychological insights with practical tactics for speaking up effectively.

Available in print, e-book, and audiobook formats.

"Choosing Courage" by Jim Detert (2021)

Based on extensive research, Detert provides frameworks for when and how to speak up effectively in workplace settings. The book includes strategies for minimizing negative consequences while maximizing positive impact.

Available from most booksellers.

"Difficult Conversations" by Douglas Stone, Bruce Patton, and Sheila Heen (2010)

While not specifically about ethics, this classic work from the Harvard Negotiation Project provides invaluable tools for navigating challenging discussions, including those about ethical concerns.

Available in multiple formats.

ARTICLES AND RESOURCES

"How to Speak Up About Ethical Issues at Work" by Amy Gallo (Harvard Business Review)

hbr.org/2015/06/how-to-speak-up-about-ethical-issues-at-work

This practical article outlines specific approaches for raising ethical concerns effectively. Available online, with limited free articles per month or through HBR subscription.

Giving Voice to Values Curriculum

givingvoicetovaluesthebook.com/curriculum

Mary Gentile's website offers free case studies and exercises for practicing how to voice and act on your values effectively in the workplace.

"Speak Up at Work" (Psychological Safety Resources)
psychsafety.co.uk/speak-up-at-work

This resource provides practical guidance for creating environments where people feel safe raising concerns. Available for free online.

INDUSTRY-SPECIFIC RESOURCES

These resources address ethical challenges in particular professional contexts.

TECHNOLOGY ETHICS

IEEE Global Initiative on Ethics of Autonomous and Intelligent Systems

standards.ieee.org/industry-connections/ec/autonomous-systems.html

For those working with AI and autonomous systems, this initiative provides principles and practical standards for ethical development and deployment. Resources are freely available online.

Ethics in Technology Practice (Markkula Center for Applied Ethics)

scu.edu/ethics/focus-areas/technology-ethics

This collection of resources addresses ethical issues in technology development and deployment. All materials are freely available online.

Montreal AI Ethics Institute

montrealethics.ai/resources

This institute offers cutting-edge research and practical resources for ethical AI development. Their "State of AI Ethics" reports provide excellent overviews of current issues.

HEALTHCARE ETHICS

American Medical Association Journal of Ethics

journalofethics.ama-assn.org

This free online journal provides case studies and resources addressing contemporary ethical issues in medicine and healthcare leadership.

National Center for Ethics in Health Care

ethics.va.gov/education

While focused on veterans' healthcare, this center offers broadly applicable ethical frameworks and training. Resources are freely available online.

Hastings Center

thehastingscenter.org/resource-library

This bioethics research institute offers resources on ethical issues in healthcare. Many resources are freely available, with more thorough access for members.

BUSINESS AND FINANCE ETHICS

"Finance Ethics" by John R. Boatright (2014)

This detailed resource addresses ethical issues specific to financial services.

Available from academic and professional booksellers.

CFA Institute Ethical Decision-Making Framework

cfainstitute.org/ethics/ethics-in-practice

While designed for investment professionals, this framework offers valuable guidance for ethical decision-making in financial contexts. Freely available online.

Sustainability Accounting Standards Board (SASB)

sasb.org

SASB provides industry-specific standards for disclosing sustainability information to investors. Their frameworks help businesses integrate ethical considerations into financial reporting.

DEVELOPING ETHICAL RESILIENCE

These resources help leaders develop the personal resilience needed to maintain ethical standards over time and through challenging situations.

BOOKS FOR BUILDING ETHICAL STRENGTH

"Moral Resilience" by Cynda Hylton Rushton (2018)

While focused on healthcare contexts, this book provides broadly applicable insights on developing the capacity to maintain moral integrity in challenging ethical situations.

Available from major booksellers.

"The Resilience Factor" by Karen Reivich and Andrew Shatte (2003)

This classic work offers practical strategies for building resilience in the face of challenges, including ethical dilemmas.

Available in print and digital formats.

"The Obstacle Is the Way" by Ryan Holiday (2014)

Drawing on ancient Stoic wisdom, Holiday provides insights on changing challenges into opportunities. His approach resonates with Daniel's ability to maintain integrity amid difficulties.

Available in multiple formats.

PODCASTS AND ONLINE RESOURCES

"Ten Percent Happier with Dan Harris"

tenpercent.com/podcast

This podcast frequently addresses resilience, values-based living, and maintaining clarity under pressure. Available on all major podcast platforms.

Greater Good Science Center

greatergood.berkeley.edu

This center provides research-based insights on well-being, compassion, and ethical resilience. Their free online magazine offers practical strategies and tools.

Center for Contemplative Mind in Society

contemplativemind.org/practices

This organization provides resources for developing contemplative practices that support ethical clarity and resilience, similar to Daniel's regular prayer practice. Resources are freely available online.

BUILDING YOUR PERSONAL ETHICAL LEADERSHIP TOOLKIT

As you explore these resources, remember that ethical leadership development is personal and ongoing. Here are some suggestions for creating your own ethical leadership toolkit:

1. **Start with what resonates.** Choose one or two resources that speak to your current challenges or interests rather than trying to absorb everything at once.
2. **Create learning rituals.** Set aside regular time, even just 15 minutes weekly, to engage with ethical leadership resources and reflect on their application to your work.
3. **Find thought partners.** Identify colleagues or mentors who share your interest in ethical leadership and discuss what you're learning together.
4. **Apply and reflect.** After engaging with a resource, identify one specific way you'll apply the insights in your work, then reflect on what happens.
5. **Build your personal resource library.** As you discover helpful resources beyond this list, add them to your personal collection.

Remember, ethical leadership isn't about having all the answers, but about developing the wisdom, courage, and resilience to navigate complex moral terrain successfully. Like Daniel, who faced unprecedented challenges throughout his career, you'll encounter situations that no resource can fully prepare you for.

In those moments, having a well-developed ethical foundation, trusted advisors, and practiced reflection skills becomes invaluable. The resources in this appendix can help you build that foundation, but in the end your own lived experience of ethical leadership will be your most powerful teacher.

May your journey of ethical leadership be both challenging and rewarding, and may you, like Daniel, discover that principled leadership creates possibilities for positive impact far beyond what you can currently imagine.

APPENDIX E: ETHICAL LEADERSHIP IN ACTION: PRACTICAL EXERCISES

INTRODUCTION

K nowledge without application remains merely information. The true power of ethical leadership emerges when we change understanding into practice, when insights become habits. This collection of exercises gives you concrete ways to develop your ethical leadership capabilities in real-world settings.

Think of these exercises as ethical leadership workouts. Just as physical fitness requires consistent practice and gradually increasing challenges, ethical leadership muscles develop through regular, intentional exercise.

Some exercises may feel uncomfortable at first. That discomfort signals growth. I encourage you to approach these exercises with both courage and patience. Choose one that resonates with your current challenges and commit to practicing it for at least two weeks before adding another. Small, consistent steps create lasting change.

As Daniel discovered through his journey from captive to cabinet minister, ethical leadership isn't developed in extraordinary moments but through consistent choices in ordinary situations. These exercises create opportunities for such choices in your daily leadership.

1. SPEAKING TRUTH TO POWER EXERCISE: THE RESPECTFUL ASSERTION PRACTICE

Before your next important meeting where you need to deliver a difficult truth, try this preparation method:

1. Write down your key message in one clear sentence.
2. Identify three specific ways this truth serves the organization's long-term interests.
3. Practice delivering your message to a trusted colleague, asking them to evaluate both your clarity and your tone.
4. Identify potential objections and prepare thoughtful responses.
5. Visualize yourself delivering the message with both respect and conviction.

Why This Works: This exercise strengthens several capabilities essential for speaking truth well. By clarifying your message and its value, you develop conviction that withstands pushback. Practicing with a colleague builds delivery skills that maintain respect while communicating difficult truths. Anticipating objections develops the agility needed for constructive dialogue.

Connection to Daniel: When Daniel interpreted the writing on the wall for King Belshazzar, he delivered an unwelcome truth about the king's reign ending. He spoke respectfully yet directly, without softening the message. Daniel's success came from his clarity, conviction, and respectful delivery, the same qualities this exercise develops.

2. CONFRONTING CORRUPTION EXERCISE: THE ETHICAL DOCUMENTATION SYSTEM

Create a structured approach for documenting potential ethical concerns:

1. Maintain a private journal of observations, recording specific behaviors or decisions that raise ethical questions.
2. Document patterns rather than isolated incidents whenever possible.
3. Note relevant policies, regulations, or values that may be compromised.
4. Record potential impacts on stakeholders, particularly the most vulnerable.
5. Outline possible constructive interventions or alternatives.

Review your documentation weekly, looking for patterns and developing thoughtful responses.

Why This Works: This exercise builds the methodical approach needed to address corruption well. By documenting patterns and impacts, you develop evidence-based perspectives that are harder to dismiss. Considering constructive alternatives changes you from critic to problem-solver, increasing your influence. The regular review develops your pattern recognition for ethical issues.

Connection to Daniel: When Daniel uncovered corruption in the Persian administration, he didn't rush to make accusations. He methodically documented patterns, gathered evidence, and developed solutions before approaching King Darius. This thoughtful preparation enabled him to address corruption constructively rather than merely pointing fingers.

3. ETHICAL DECISION-MAKING IN HOSTILE ENVIRONMENTS EXERCISE: THE VALUES CLARIFICATION MAP

When facing pressure to compromise your values:

1. Draw a circle in the center of a page and write your name in it.
2. Around this circle, draw smaller circles containing each stakeholder affected by your decision.
3. For each stakeholder, note their interests, concerns, and potential impact on them.
4. Now draw another circle containing your core values relevant to this situation.
5. Draw lines between values and stakeholders where they align.
6. Identify where stakeholder interests conflict with your values.
7. Develop approaches that honor your non-negotiable values while addressing legitimate stakeholder concerns.

Why This Works: This exercise clarifies complex ethical dilemmas visually, making competing pressures and potential alignments visible. By mapping connections between values and stakeholders, you often discover unexpected areas of alignment. This visual approach activates different cognitive processes than linear thinking, revealing creative solutions that honor integrity while respecting legitimate concerns.

Connection to Daniel: When Morgan Hayes faced pressure to approve an environmentally devastating project, she experienced the same tension Daniel felt between organizational expectations and deeper values. This mapping exercise helps modern leaders achieve what Morgan did: identifying which values are truly non-negotiable while finding creative ways to address legitimate organizational concerns.

4. STANDING FIRM WHEN POWER DEMANDS COMPROMISE EXERCISE: THE BOUNDARY CLARIFICATION PRACTICE

For this exercise, identify an area where you feel pressure to compromise:

1. Write a clear statement of your ethical boundary in positive terms ("I am committed to..." rather than "I won't...").
2. For this boundary, create three tiers:

- Tier 1: Absolutely non-negotiable under any circumstances
- Tier 2: Strong preference, would require exceptional circumstances to reconsider
- Tier 3: Flexible, depending on context and competing values

3. For your Tier 1 boundaries, develop two alternative approaches that maintain your boundary while addressing legitimate concerns others might have.
4. Practice articulating both your boundary and creative alternatives until they feel natural.

Why This Works: This exercise changes vague discomfort into clear ethical boundaries. By distinguishing between absolute and flexible boundaries, you develop precise ethical thinking. Developing alternatives while maintaining core boundaries builds the creative problem-solving essential for ethical leadership in complex organizations.

Connection to Daniel: When presented with food that violated his dietary commitments, Daniel didn't simply refuse or reluctantly comply. He proposed a creative alternative that respected his boundaries while addressing his supervisor's legitimate concerns about his health and appearance. This exercise helps you develop similar creative responses to ethical pressure.

5. NAVIGATING ETHICAL GRAY AREAS EXERCISE: THE ETHICAL PERSPECTIVE EXPANSION

When facing a situation with no clear right answer:

1. Identify the key ethical values or principles in tension.
2. Take five minutes to write the strongest case you can for perspective A.
3. Take another five minutes to write the strongest case for perspective B.
4. For each perspective, identify its:

- Core legitimate concerns
- Potential unintended consequences
- Underlying assumptions

5. Based on this analysis, develop an approach that honors the legitimate concerns of both perspectives.

Why This Works: This exercise combats our natural tendency toward binary thinking and confirmation bias. By deliberately taking opposing perspectives, you develop the cognitive flexibility needed for ethical gray areas. Identifying legitimate concerns on all sides leads to more multifaceted solutions that balance competing values rather than sacrificing one entirely.

Connection to Daniel: Throughout his career, Daniel demonstrated remarkable ability to navigate competing priorities without compromising core principles. When addressing corruption in Persian governance, he balanced justice against political realities, accountability against mercy. This exercise develops the same balanced wisdom Daniel exemplified.

6. ETHICS OF LOYALTY AND JUSTICE EXERCISE: THE LOYALTY HIERARCHY ASSESSMENT

When experiencing conflicting loyalties:

1. List all entities to whom you feel loyalty in this situation (organization, team, profession, society, specific individuals, principles, etc.).
2. Rank these loyalties from highest to lowest based on your deeply held values, not immediate pressures.
3. For each loyalty, answer:

- What does this loyalty require of me in this situation?
- What greater purpose does this loyalty serve?
- How might I honor this loyalty while still respecting others?

4. Identify where loyalties conflict and where they might actually reinforce each other.

5. Based on your hierarchy and analysis, articulate your path forward.

Why This Works: This exercise changes vague feelings of conflicting obligations into structured ethical reasoning. By explicitly ranking loyalties, you develop clarity about your true priorities. Examining the purpose behind each loyalty often reveals shared underlying values that create unexpected alignment possibilities.

Connection to Daniel: When faced with a decree forbidding prayer to anyone but the king, Daniel had to navigate competing loyalties to his God, his king, and his professional responsibilities. His clarity about loyalty hierarchy enabled him to maintain respect for the king while honoring his highest loyalty. This exercise develops similar clarity for modern loyalty conflicts.

7. CRISIS LEADERSHIP EXERCISE: THE ETHICAL CRISIS SIMULATION

With your team or trusted colleagues:

1. Create a realistic crisis scenario relevant to your organization that would test ethical commitments (resource scarcity, time pressure, competing stakeholder demands).
2. Establish roles, including observers who will provide feedback.
3. Simulate the crisis in real time for 20-30 minutes, making decisions under pressure.
4. After the simulation, discuss:

- Which values were most difficult to maintain under pressure?
- What decision-making processes emerged in crisis?
- How might you strengthen ethical clarity for future crises?

5. Create a one-page ethical crisis protocol based on your insights.

Why This Works: This exercise develops the ethical muscle memory needed when crisis strikes. Real-time simulation reveals how pressure affects your decision-making in ways intellectual discussion cannot. By identifying vulnerabilities before actual crisis, you can develop protocols and practices that maintain ethical clarity when it matters most.

Connection to Daniel: Throughout Jerusalem's siege, Jeremiah demonstrated ethical leadership under extreme pressure, balancing practical guidance with unwavering moral clarity. This exercise helps modern leaders develop similar capabilities before crisis strikes, preparing them to maintain integrity even under the severest pressure.

8. MODERN APPLICATION OF ANCIENT WISDOM EXERCISE: THE ETHICAL TRADITION BRIDGE

Select a contemporary ethical challenge you're facing:

1. Research how three different wisdom traditions (from different cultures or time periods) might approach this challenge.
2. For each tradition, identify:

- Core principles relevant to your situation

- How these principles were applied in their original context
- How principles might translate to your contemporary context

3. Look for areas of convergence across traditions.
4. Create a personal approach that honors timeless wisdom while addressing modern realities.

Why This Works: This exercise breaks us out of presentism—the assumption that our challenges are entirely unique and unprecedented. By connecting with ethical wisdom across cultures and time periods, you develop both humility and creativity. Identifying convergence across traditions often reveals enduring principles that transcend cultural and historical contexts.

Connection to Daniel: When Dr. Evelyn Lancaster applied Daniel's ethical framework to AI development at Quantum Dynamics, she demonstrated how ancient wisdom can illuminate cutting-edge technological challenges. This exercise helps you develop the same ability to extract timeless principles and apply them to contemporary situations.

9. ETHICAL RESILIENCE EXERCISE: THE ETHICAL REFLECTION JOURNAL

Create a journal with these three columns:

1. Situation: Describe an ethically challenging situation you faced.
2. Response: Record how you responded in the moment.
3. Reflection: Evaluate your response against your core values and consider alternative approaches.

Commit to making at least three entries per week. Monthly, review your journal to identify patterns in your ethical responses and areas for growth.

Why This Works: This exercise develops the self-awareness essential for ethical resilience. Regular reflection changes reactive ethical responses into thoughtful patterns. By documenting your ethical journey, you create accountability to yourself and develop awareness of your growth over time. The practice of considering alternatives builds flexibility for future challenges.

Connection to Daniel: Daniel maintained consistent spiritual practices that renewed his moral compass regardless of external circumstances. His daily prayer discipline wasn't just religious observance but ethical renewal. This journaling practice creates a similar renewal rhythm for modern leaders facing complex pressures.

10. INTEGRATION: THE DANIEL FRAMEWORK IN PRACTICE
EXERCISE: THE ETHICAL LEADERSHIP SCENARIOS WORKSHOP

With colleagues or your team:

1. Create 5-7 realistic ethical scenarios relevant to your organization or industry.
2. For each scenario, apply the DANIEL Framework:

- Define the ethical issue
- Analyze the context
- Navigate competing loyalties
- Investigate alternatives
- Evaluate long-term consequences
- Lead with moral courage

3. Compare different approaches and discuss what you learn from the framework's application.
4. Identify which steps in the framework prove most challenging for your team.
5. Create specific strategies to strengthen those challenging areas.

Why This Works: This exercise changes the DANIEL Framework from abstract concept to practical tool through application to relevant scenarios. By working through multiple situations, you develop pattern recognition for ethical challenges. Identifying challenging framework steps reveals growth opportunities specific to your team or organization.

Connection to Daniel: The DANIEL Framework distills the essence of Daniel's approach to ethical leadership across multiple situations. This exercise helps you internalize these principles so deeply that they become instinctive, just as Daniel's ethical principles guided him through decades of service across changing regimes and circumstances.

CONCLUSION: FROM EXERCISE TO CHANGE

These exercises aren't merely academic activities but invitations to changed leadership. As you incorporate them into your regular practice, you'll likely notice several shifts:

First, your ethical awareness will sharpen. You'll recognize ethical dimensions of situations earlier, before pressure intensifies and options narrow.

Second, your response agility will increase. Rather than freezing or defaulting to expedient choices under pressure, you'll access a wider range of creative approaches.

Third, your influence will expand. As others observe your consistent ethical leadership, they'll increasingly seek your guidance on complex issues.

Finally, your leadership legacy will deepen. Beyond immediate results, you'll shape organizational cultures and develop future ethical leaders whose impact extends far beyond what you can currently imagine.

Like Daniel, whose influence transcended his immediate context and continues to inspire ethical leadership millennia later, your commitment to developing these ethical leadership capabilities creates ripples of impact far beyond what you can currently see.

The journey of ethical leadership isn't about achieving perfection but about consistent growth. Each exercise you practice builds capacity for the next challenge. Each small choice of integrity creates momentum for larger stands. In this way, ordinary leadership moments become opportunities for extraordinary impact.

Which exercise will you begin practicing today?

NOTE FROM THE AUTHOR
THANK YOU FOR YOUR INVESTMENT IN GROWTH

Dear Reader,

Thank you for investing your valuable time in this book. I trust that these insights and principles have provided you with practical tools for your personal, professional, or spiritual journey.

Your engagement with this material means a great deal, and I'd be grateful if you'd consider sharing your experience with others. Would you take a moment to leave an honest review? Your feedback not only helps others discover these resources but also contributes to our collective growth and learning.

Your insights can be shared on any of these platforms:

📚Amazon   Goodreads

Want to stay connected? I'd love to keep you updated on new releases and exclusive content:

- Subscribe to insights
- Access free resources: LeadAIEthically.com JournalingInsights.com RichardFrench.Net

With appreciation for your commitment to growth,

Richard French

ABOUT THE AUTHOR

Richard French stands at the intersection of technological innovation and ethical leadership. One of the country's foremost authorities on Robotic Process Automation and AI, French has been a driving force behind several companies that have reshaped the business landscape. His career, which includes executive roles at Oracle and Nokia and CEO positions at several successful startups, has been defined by a commitment to ethical decision-making in rapid technological change.

French's expertise spans various technologies, from software and mobile applications to AI and automation. He has led organizations on five continents, navigating the complex ethical terrain of global business expansion. Throughout his career, French has demonstrated that ethical leadership and business success are not mutually exclusive. His philosophy that "people work with us, not for us" has been instrumental in building ethical, high-performing teams in diverse cultural contexts.

Trained as a mathematician, French brings an analytical mind to the often ambiguous world of business ethics. He has a talent for breaking down complex ethical dilemmas into manageable frameworks, a skill that has made him a sought-after speaker and board member. French's ethical leadership approach is moral and practical, informed by years of making high-stakes decisions in competitive business environments.

In addition to his professional accomplishments, French is an accomplished GT racing driver. This pursuit has sharpened his understanding of the importance of split-second decisions and the balance between risk and responsibility lessons he applies to business ethics.

In Daniel as a Blueprint for Navigating Ethical Dilemmas (2nd Edition), French draws on his vast experience to bridge the gap between ancient wisdom and modern ethical challenges. Combining timeless principles with contemporary case studies, he offers readers a unique and powerful approach to ethical leadership in the 21st century.

ALSO BY RICHARD FRENCH

PROVERBS
— FOR —
PROFIT

ANCIENT WISDOM FOR
MODERN BUSINESS ETHICS

RICHARD FRENCH

REVELATION EXPLAINED

RICHARD FRENCH

THE Art OF JOURNALING

A COMPREHENSIVE GUIDE TO WRITING A JOURNAL

RICHARD FRENCH

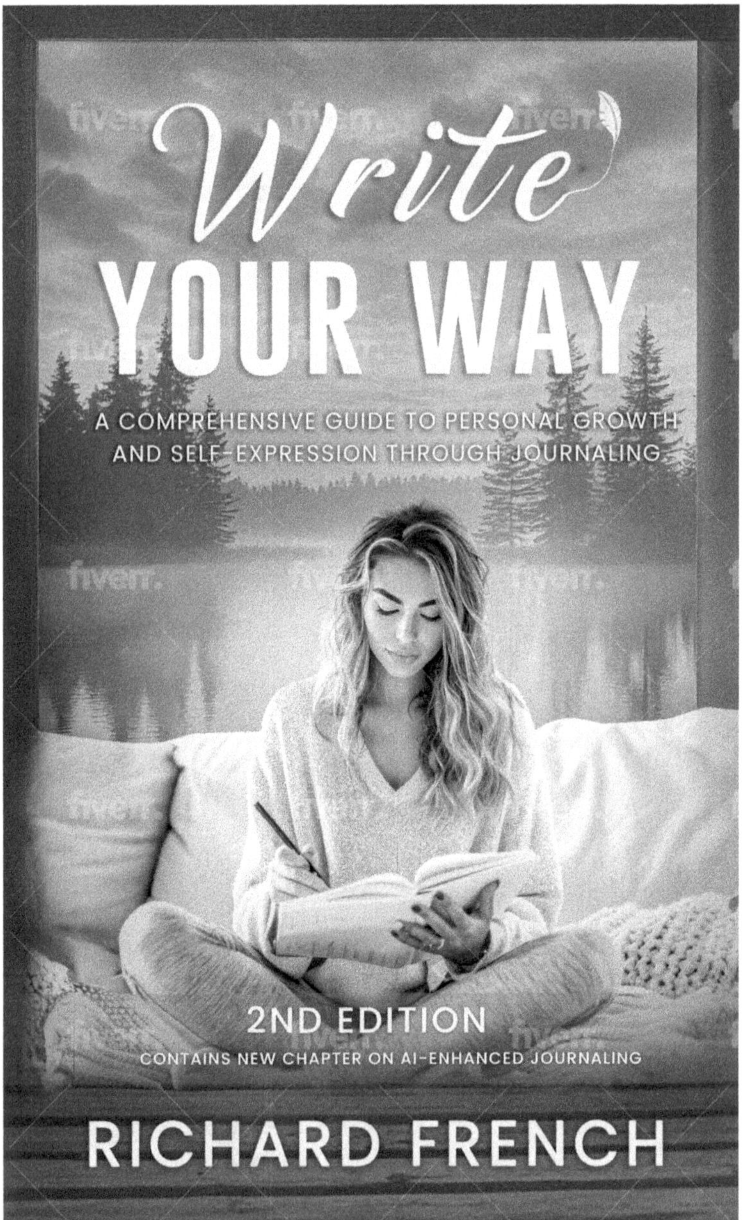
Write
YOUR WAY
A COMPREHENSIVE GUIDE TO PERSONAL GROWTH
AND SELF-EXPRESSION THROUGH JOURNALING
2ND EDITION
CONTAINS NEW CHAPTER ON AI-ENHANCED JOURNALING
RICHARD FRENCH

THE YEAR-END
REFLECTION
GUIDE

A WRITE YOUR WAY JOURNALING BONUS

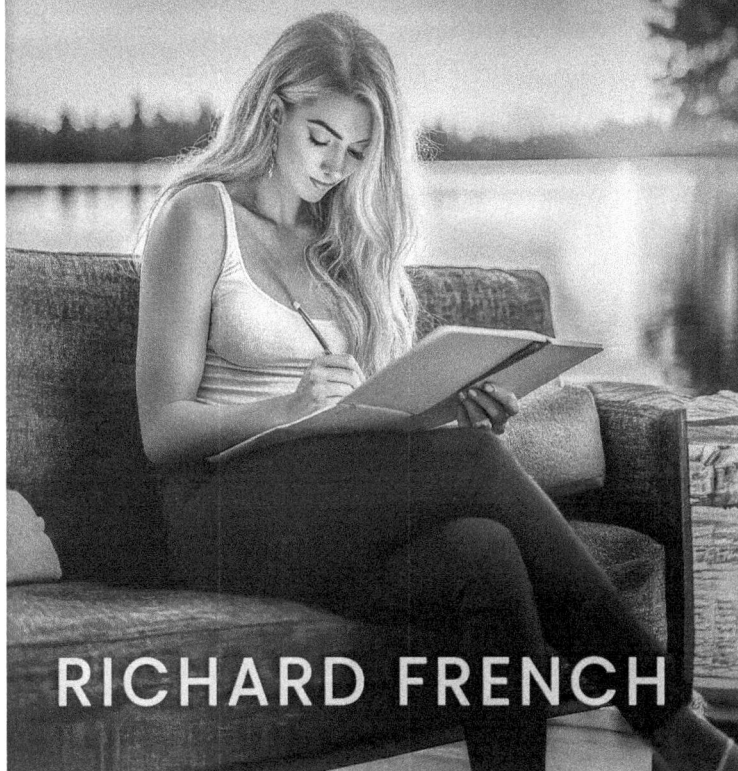

RICHARD FRENCH

ADVANCED PATTERN RECOGNITION

AN ART OF JOURNALING BONUS GUIDE

RICHARD FRENCH

100
SELF-DISCOVERY
JOURNALING PROMPTS

RICHARD FRENCH

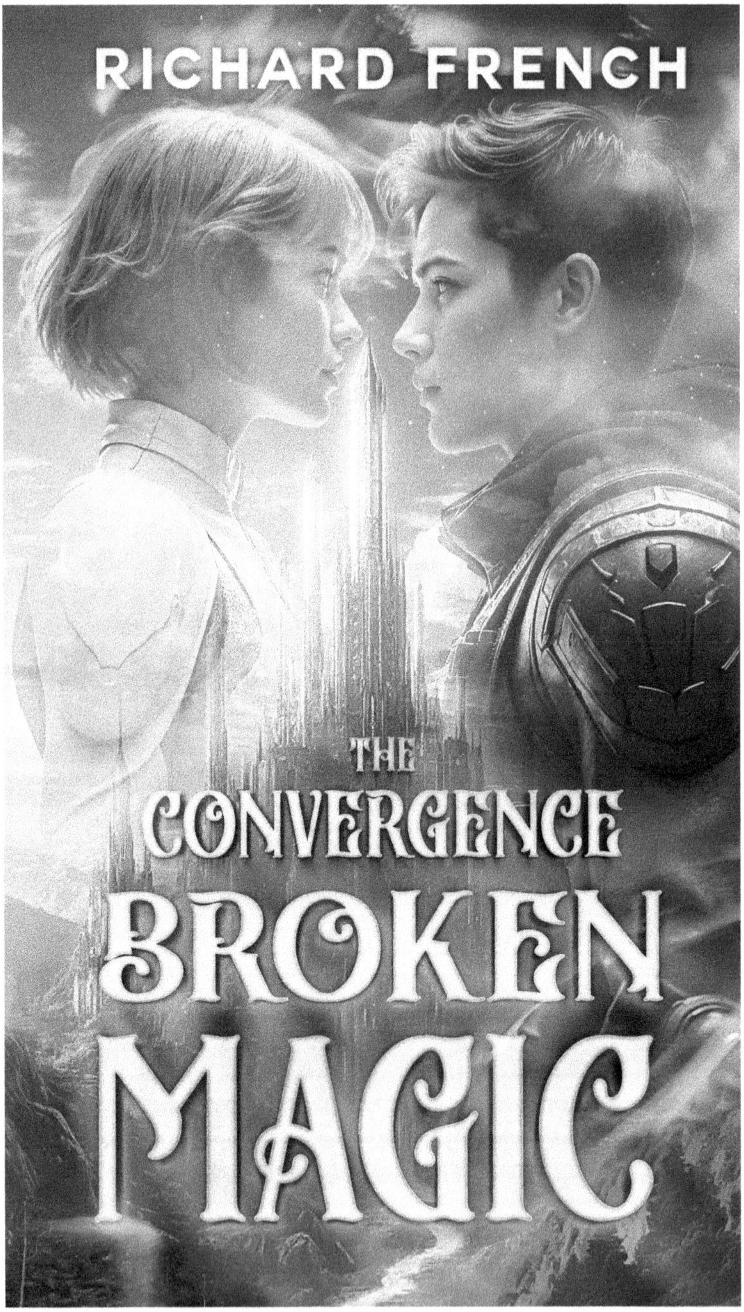
RICHARD FRENCH
THE
CONVERGENCE
BROKEN
MAGIC